Finding Purpose
in
NARNIA

Finding Purpose
in
NARNIA

A Journey with Prince Caspian

GINA BURKART

HiddenSpring

Cover design by Sharyn Banks
Book design by Lynn Else

Library of Congress Cataloging-in-Publication Data

Burkart, Gina, 1971–
    Finding purpose in Narnia : a journey with Prince Caspian / Gina Burkart.
        p. cm.
    Includes bibliographical references.
    ISBN-13: 978-1-58768-028-1 (alk. paper)
    1. Lewis, C. S. (Clive Staples), 1898–1963. Prince Caspian. 2. Children's stories, English—History and criticism. 3. Christian fiction, English—History and criticism. 4. Fantasy fiction, English—History and criticism. 5. Narnia (Imaginary place) 6. Spirituality in literature. I. Title.
    PR6023.E926P76326 2008
    823'.912—dc22

                                 2007050571

Published by
HiddenSpring
an imprint of Paulist Press
997 Macarthur Boulevard
Mahwah, New Jersey 07430

www.hiddenspringbooks.com

Printed and bound in the
United States of America

CONTENTS

SECTION ONE: **Finding Faith**

Passing on Great Stories . . . 3
Prince Caspian longs for Old Narnia and wants to hear the stories from Doctor Cornelius.

Believing in What We Can't See . . . 10
Susan struggles with following Lucy because she can't see Aslan.

Returning to Days Past . . . 20
The Pevensie children return to Narnia to learn more lessons. They are pulled back when they least expect it.

Growing Out of Imagination . . . 26
Susan and Peter learn that they will not return to Narnia because they will become too old.

The Myth of Power . . . 33
Nikabrik believes the White Witch is more powerful than Aslan.

Being Called . . . 41
Prince Caspian is called from his sleep by Doctor Cornelius— much like Samuel.

Getting Lost . . . 45
The children get lost in their attempts to find the Stone Table.

Closed Doors . . . 51
Reepicheep volunteers to go through the door. Aslan tells him it will not be in his best interest.

CONTENTS

SECTION TWO: **Holding on to Hope**

CONTENTS

SECTION THREE: **Learning to Love**

ACKNOWLEDGMENTS

I thank my mom and dad for encouraging me to imagine and wonder. They opened my eyes to see the grace of God at work all around me. I also thank them for endlessly answering my questions and for never tiring of reading to me and with me.

I thank my husband for listening to and sharing my dreams. His love gives me a glimpse of God's love.

I thank my children for helping me to see this world through the eyes of a child. They never cease to amaze me with their wisdom.

I also thank my cousin, Laura. When we were children, she loved Narnia more than anyone I knew. I also thank her for reading this book in its early stages and giving me encouragement and suggestions.

Above all, I thank God for guiding me each day in faith, hope, and love. To him, I give all credit for this book.

INTRODUCTION

What I love about reading C. S. Lewis's Narnia tales is that he never lets us forget what it is like to be a child. When I was a child, these stories spoke to me on my own level. They understood me and pulled me in so that I felt understood. In Narnia I was able to work through my fears and struggles.

Although I loved all of the characters and adventures, I was particularly fond of the Pevensie children. They first took me to Narnia, and it was with them that I fought the White Witch, met Aslan, and had my first taste of Turkish delight.

When I was pulled back with them to meet Prince Caspian, I rejoiced to see Aslan again and made friendships with the creatures of Old Narnia. However, as I read this story as an adult, I marvel at how C. S. Lewis connects us with the lessons of scripture. In particular, he brings to life the verse of 1 Corinthians 13:13.

While that verse binds together the theological virtues of faith, hope, and love and tells us that the greatest is love, Lewis connects these virtues to our everyday struggles. He personifies the virtues through his entire story in a way that helps us to understand.

The three sections of this book show the journey of C. S. Lewis and how his works relate to scripture. I connect him with the fictional character of Prince Caspian so that you may see how Lewis found purpose in Narnia and hoped that his readers would as well. I also share my own experiences and memories. In the following pages may you also come to find faith, hope, and love in Narnia.

SECTION ONE
FINDING FAITH

It [love] bears all things, believes all things…
1 Corinthians 13:7

Passing on Great Stories

Reflections on Lewis with Caspian

*A*fter reading *Surprised by Joy*, I found much of Lewis in Narnia and perhaps saw him emerge as the young Prince Caspian. In getting to know Caspian, we get many glimpses of Lewis as a boy who remains forever young in Narnia. As we know, once a king in Narnia, always a king in Narnia.

In the scene where young Caspian rises out of bed and looks up at the stars with Doctor Cornelius, we also may envision Lewis looking at his toy garden created in the lid of a biscuit tin. In *Surprised by Joy*, he tells us that the toy garden created by his brother first made him notice nature. Looking back years later in writing his autobiography, Lewis realized that this garden "stirred his imagination" and formed his idea of what paradise must be like. You can almost see him now playing with the garden in his nursery, as he looks out the window at the "Green Hills" that "taught [him] longing."[1] This seems to be the same longing that Caspian displayed for Narnia as he looked at the stars and listened intently to Doctor Cornelius.

This early memory became so ingrained in Lewis that years later when standing "beside a flowering current bush" (remind you of Moses?) it "suddenly arose in [him] without warning."[2] Although Lewis finds it difficult "to find words strong enough for the sensation," he compares it to Milton's "enormous bliss of Eden."[3] He tells us that "it was a sensation of desire" that fleeted as soon as it had arrived. He was left stirred by "a longing for the longing that ceased."[4]

Those of us who have also experienced this stirring and longing that Lewis describes may identify these sensations as the soul's longing to be reunited in paradise with God. When our mind often fails to direct us, our inner longings often lead. We just need to recognize them and follow.

At an early age, Lewis's inner being had been moved by a toy garden. He felt an unknowing longing for the paradise that Adam and Eve had found in Eden. Later, it appears that he worked this longing out through the character of Caspian who yearns for the past days of Narnia. With Caspian, we listen intently to the stories of Doctor Cornelius and travel to Narnia to bring the past days of paradise back to the present.

Personal Ponderings

A Dance of the Past and Present

In his autobiography, Lewis tells us that in his home he was surrounded with "endless books....There were books in the study, books in the drawing room, books in the cloakroom, books (two deep) in the great bookcase on the landing, books in a bedroom, books piled as high as my shoulder in the cistern attic, books of all kinds."[5] I can easily relate to this. Like Lewis, I find they reach out to me, and I embrace them. Lovingly turning the pages, characters speak, scenes unfold, and images are permanently painted and stored in one's personal gallery. From time to time, we revisit this gallery and use it to make meaning from life.

As Lewis's father fueled his love of reading, my mother passed this habit on to me. When I was little, she would sit on the couch and wait for me to pile up all my books into a tower at her feet. I would sit snuggled in my favorite burgundy and purple plaid blanket while she patiently passed the afternoon reading every book from my pile. I had my mom, my blanket, and my books. Life could not be better. Securely, I sat back and listened as the stories unfolded.

As I grew older, I learned to read on my own. This reading activity had to be shared, so I brought out all the dolls and stuffed animals from my toy box and lined them up beside me on the couch, and covered all of us in my blanket. At my side sat a pile of books. I spent the afternoon reading the stories aloud to my captive audience, ever so often stopping to ask what they thought about the story.

This memory came back to me recently while conversing in my gallery with Caspian and Doctor Cornelius. I listened with Caspian in earnest of Narnia's history and wished that I could also talk to the animals of the forest. I got out of bed with them in the dark of the night and "followed the Doctor through many passages and up several staircases."[6] I climbed excitedly "up the dark winding stair of the tower."[7] At the top of the tower, all three of us looked at the two stars that "hung rather low in the southern sky, almost as bright as two little moons and very close together."[8] As we gazed in awe and listened to the distant roar of the waterfall at Beaversdam, Caspian and I wondered, "Are they ever going to have a collision?"[9] Wisely, Doctor Cornelius whispered back to us, "Nay…the great lords of the upper sky know the steps of their dance too well for that. Look well upon them. Their meeting is fortunate and means some great good for the sad realm of Narnia."[10]

Reflecting on the stars, Doctor Cornelius's words whispered: The memories of my past dance are with me in the present as they illuminate a brighter future—like the Pevensie children came from the present to meet Caspian in the past to shape the future of Narnia.

A Captive Audience—of a King and Queens?

My mother's tradition of reading has continued with my own children—a "king" and two "queens." Through our stories, we have come to share our lives. The characters of the stories have led us to understanding.

My mother very wisely made this tradition richer and fuller by introducing me to the Bible and the lives of the saints. She knew that in order to understand my present, I needed to know my past. The Bible gave me my history and identity.

One sees Doctor Cornelius relaying to Caspian his heritage and connection to Narnia. Caspian eagerly listens as Cornelius tells him, "All you have heard about Old Narnia is true. It is not the land of men. It is the country of Aslan, the country of the Waking Trees and Visible Niads, of Fauns, and Satyrs..."[11] This conversation gives way to the words of my mother: "What you read in the Bible is true. It is not the word of man; it is the word of God. In it you meet angels, prophets, saints, sinners, demons, and the Son of God."

Sometimes my mother would let us carefully look through her family Bible after she read from it. Inside, its golden-edged pages with bright colorful scenes brought the Bible mysteries to life. What I loved best about that Bible, what made it special, was that it had been my grandparents. On the cover was written my family history. They had read from it to my mother and her siblings, just as she was reading from it to us.

As I touched the pages, I got chills knowing that my grandfather who died long before I was born had touched those same pages. He had heard about God from the same pages I was hearing about him. Through those pages, I felt my grandfather's presence. I felt our connection even though we had never met—like two stars meeting in a dark sky—past and present dancing to bring about some good in the future.

Once again, listen to Doctor Cornelius's voice as he relates his two reasons for sharing stories of the past:

> Firstly, because my old heart has carried these secret memories so long that it aches with them and would burst if it would not whisper them to you. But secondly for this: that when you become King you may help us, for I know that you also…love the Old Things.[12]

Reading to our children and sharing our faith with them has long been part of family histories. Through this activity, we learn to love literature, grow in our faith, and most importantly get a sense of self-identity—from where I came, who I am, and who I need to be. Like Doctor Cornelius, our hearts are longing to share our secret memories, faith, and love for stories with our children. This sharing of stories connects us and shapes our future. In a society seemingly preoccupied with anything that is new, children who are our future need to be taught to "love the old things."

Finding Purpose

What traditions meant the most to you as a child?

Who passed on these traditions to you?

How do your traditions show the dance between the past and present?

How can they shape the future?

How do you pass on your present and past to others?

What is your dance?

Who are the kings and queens you are inviting to your dance?

Finding Scripture

It is not a coincidence that most families have etched their family trees inside the pages of their Bible. Although it may have been a cherished family heirloom passed down through the generations, the Bible also held the early accounts of where it all began. Our faith passed through the Old Testament families and into the New Testament families. We are all connected as members of God's family and cannot tell the stories of our heritage without including our struggles and trials told in the Bible.

As my mother shared the family Bible with me and I lovingly touched the pages my grandfather and grandmother had touched before me, I also felt the energy of the stories the pages held. I knew that my ancestors had also found faith, hope, and love in the scriptures. I knew that they also found refuge from daily life in those pages. In the Bible they found a connection to their ancestors in the same way that I was connecting with them—a connection that could be traced to the beginning of time. In learning about God and his coming into this world as Christ, we are connected with our larger faith family.

The Dance of the Old and New

Lewis subtly calls our attention to the dance of the old and new through Doctor Cornelius and Caspian. While looking up and reflecting on the stars with them, we think about our own family stars. Yet, we also are reminded of the star that led three wise men to discover a newborn infant that fulfilled the Old Testament prophesies. In the birth of Christ, we have "the perfect dance of the Old and the New."

Looking upon this star brings one back to the Gospel of Matthew. Remember how a star led the Magi from the East to find

Herod in Jerusalem and inquire, "Where is the child who has been born king of the Jews? For we observed his star at its rising, and have come to pay him homage" (Matt 2:2). Lewis uses the star in this scene symbolically for it was a common ancient belief that new stars appeared to indicate a ruler's birth. Lewis's purpose here is twofold. In addition to foreshadowing that Caspian will be the new ruler of Narnia, he also calls us to contemplate how Christ fulfilled the prophesies of the Old Testament to give us a new relationship with God. We are reminded in Matthew that God had promised to send a ruler "to shepherd [God's] people Israel" and that the ruler would come from Bethlehem (Matt 2:6).

In this scene, Lewis takes us back to reflect on how our great and awesome Lord of the Dance came into this world as a helpless infant to invite us to an eternal dance that will never end. In this dance, we are all connected, for one day our Lord will reunite all of his faithful family in a celebratory dance in heaven.

Suggested Scripture Reading and Reflections

Read the infancy narrative of Matthew 1—2. Consider how this narrative brings together the past and future to direct you in the present.

How is this narrative reminiscent of the story of Moses and the exile from Egypt?

Mary and Joseph were well instructed in the scripture of the Old Testament. How did this give them strength and courage during their own exile?

How might they have found faith in the story of Moses?

Why is it important to reflect on the connection of past, present, and future?

How can you draw on your scriptural heritage to grow in your daily faith struggles?

What lessons have been passed on to you from your ancestors?

Believing in What We Can't See

Reflections on Lewis with Caspian

*I*n *Surprised by Joy,* Lewis tells us of his own journey through spiritual darkness. His autobiography reveals that he spent many years of his life lost. Although he had glimpses of joy that filled him with a longing, he "in vain" wasted much of his life with "waitings and watchings for Joy."[13] He explains that he later learned that while the joy he experienced led him "into the region of awe," this region is not "clothed in the senses."[14] Rather, he describes this desire as a kind of "love."[15]

Furthermore, Lewis explains that while most of us look at ourselves as "mortals, seen as the sciences see us," we can better understand ourselves, as we really are: "appearances of the Absolute...which is the utter reality."[16] In the following scene from *Prince Caspian,* Lewis uses Lucy to show us what type of seeing is required to lead ourselves out of the spiritual darkness he experienced. Unlike the other characters, Lucy sees with her heart and inner being. This type of seeing leads her to Aslan. The other characters, in relying on their physical sense of sight, ignore the inner longings. Thus, they remain lost until they learn to let go of their physical senses and listen to the yearnings of their heart. Likewise, they ignore Lucy and refuse to follow her lead. Had they seen her as "an appearance of the absolute" and a spiritual guide, they would have found their way much sooner. Through the following scene,

Lucy teaches us to see and listen with our hearts. This type of seeing will show us God's presence in our surroundings and others.

But I Can't See Him!

Not surprisingly, Aslan appears to Lucy first. She is able to see him when the others do not. Little children have an innocence about them that allows them to see and feel what others cannot. They trust in what seems impossible. As we age, we lose this childlike faith. We begin to trust more in the tested and proven. We rely on our five senses to understand the world.

Lewis illustrates this beautifully in the scene where Aslan first appears to Lucy.

> "Look! Look! Look!" cried Lucy.
> "Where? What?" said everyone.
> "The Lion," said Lucy. "Aslan himself. Didn't you see?" Her face had changed completely and her eyes shone.
> "Do you really mean—?" began Peter.
> "Where did you think you saw him?" asked Susan.
> "Don't talk like a grown-up," said Lucy, stamping her foot. "I didn't think I saw him. I saw him."[17]

Susan and Peter really struggle with this. They want to believe Lucy, but they cannot see Aslan, and Lucy is the youngest. How can they believe in what they cannot see? Susan uses the word "think" to imply that Lucy may have only thought she saw Aslan. Lucy blasts Susan with, "Don't talk like a grown-up." This statement is meant for all of us. We think too much and second-guess what we know to be true. Lucy confidently trusts what she saw. She trusts her instincts and her heart.

Like Susan, Lewis also struggled with this type of thinking. Greatly influenced by literature and philosophy, Lewis spent much of his life intellectually reasoning about why he should or should not believe. Even after Chesterton's "Christian outline of history" in *Everlasting Man* "seemed to make sense" and one of "the hardest boiled of all atheists...on the other side of the fire...remarked that the evidence of the historicity of the Gospels was really surprisingly good,"[18] Lewis found himself unmoved. He tells us that it was not until he was corrected by his friends Owen Barfield and Alan Griffiths that he discovered he had been thinking about faith in the wrong manner.

In a conversation where he referred to philosophy as "a subject," Barfield remarked, "It wasn't a *subject* to Plato; it was a way."[19] Lewis tells us that this remark with the "quiet but fervent agreement of Griffths, and the quick glance of agreement between these two, revealed to [him his] own frivolity....It was time that something should be done."[20] Lewis then goes on to tell us this meant, "All my acts, desires, and thoughts were to be brought into harmony with universal Spirit. For the first time I examined myself with a seriously practical purpose."[21]

In the aforementioned scene, Lucy has that purpose. She listens and follows the spirit working within her. Susan ignores that spirit and Lucy. Instead, she relies on her intellect and reason. Like Lewis, this keeps her from doing what really needs to be done. Through the interaction of Susan and Lucy, Lewis attempts to show us the errors of his own ways. In this scene of Narnia, he wants us to find our purpose—as he finally did. Lucy in her childlike innocence recognizes and follows her purpose. Susan in her "grown-up" thinking seems to have become lost.

Personal Ponderings

The Big Question

Seeing God preoccupies all of us. Like Lewis, many of us spend much time trying to see God with our physical sense of eyesight. However, like Lewis, we find that this is impossible. My first memory of struggling with this begins at the age of four.

When my mother told me that we were each fashioned and molded by God in his image, thoughts emerged of God's fingers delicately forming the features of my face and shaping my arms, legs, and hands. I tried to remember what that felt like and what his breath smelled like when he blew life into me and gave me a soul. What did he think of me? What did he say to me? What did God sound like? Did he name me before my parents did? Most importantly, what did God look like?

Pondering and reflecting on God creating me conjured up further images of once living in heaven and playing with the angels. Imagine jumping up and down in the clouds with angel playmates and living in big cloud houses where play and fun were endless. However, I could not remember what God looked like, and that really bothered me. How could I not see God's face?

Sitting in an empty lot beside my house, digging with a spoon I had sneaked out of the kitchen, I decided to pose my question to my playmates, since they, too, were also created by God and came from heaven. This seemed the perfect opportunity, as we were only at the yellow clay in the hole we were digging. We never went beyond the red clay because that meant we were getting too close to hell and the devil, and we were still a few colors above the red.

When questioning my friends about God making us of clay, sending us to earth, and not remembering what God looked like, they kept on digging and became very quiet. Finally, one of my friends spoke. She inquired: "He did? I do not remember that. I didn't know we were in heaven." Another friend said: "That's because we weren't. She is such a liar. We came out of our mommy's tummy." Tossing down the spoon with disbelief, the hole did not matter anymore since my friend called me a liar. The thought of getting my mother to resolve this dispute crossed my mind.

The hole of dirt did not get any deeper. There was no threat of red clay that day. Instead began the big black hole that finds us all: If God made us, who made God? Many of us grapple with the answer; God always was and will be.

Lewis also found himself in this quandary shortly after discovering that he needed "to be brought into harmony with the universal Spirit," he tells us that once his "philosophical theorem...stood upright and became a living presence," he found that it "waived the point" and "would not argue about it. He only said, 'I am Lord'; 'I am that I am'; 'I am.'"[22]

This mystery requires a faith that challenges us all. Because we depend so much on our physical senses, we grapple with what we cannot see, hear, touch, taste, and smell. Like Susan, we question and sometimes refuse to believe in what we cannot see.

Seeing God

Seeing God in our daily lives requires a different kind of sight. It means we should open up to the extraordinary and look at the big picture. This requires us to think about how we are all connected. Unfortunately, sometimes it takes tragedies such as September 11, hurricane Katrina, and the southeast Pacific tsunami to teach us these lessons.

For many years, I looked for that really big "wow" experience where I could say, "That was him! God looks like _____." Now I realize that looking too hard blinded me from really seeing that God has always been there and always will be there. The gaze of a young child, the smile of a stranger, and the unexpected hug of a loved one are just a few ways that God wraps his arms around us and embraces us with his unconditional love and acceptance.

Lewis touches upon this when he realizes that we are all "appearances" of God. As appearances of God, created in his image, do we not reflect God to one another in our words and actions? Like Lucy, can we not also be spiritual guides for one another?

Lewis's description of his first experience of Oxford personifies this understanding. Getting off the train, he becomes disappointed with the "succession of mean shops." He continues walking "always expecting the next turn to reveal the beauties,"[23] but not until he gets to the open country does he turn around and look behind himself. Then he sees "far away, never more beautiful since...the fabled cluster of spires and towers." He realizes then that he exited the station on the "wrongside,"[24] and later sees this as an allegory for his own life. Could this also be true of us? Could we in our physical attempts to see God be looking at life from the wrong side?

Susan and Peter do this too. Being so eager to see Aslan, they looked too hard. Instead of tapping into their instincts and hearts, they try to rely on their senses. This blinds them. When we ignore our inner feelings, we blind ourselves. As they continue on their journey in the dark, they have to rely on their instincts rather than their sight. They need to follow Lucy and trust that Aslan is leading Lucy. When they finally stop trying to see with their eyes and look with their hearts, they begin to see from the right side and begin to see Aslan.

The same is true for us. When we tap into our inner feelings and instincts, we find God. When the children really quiz Lucy about how she knows she saw Aslan, she confidently responds "He—I—I—just know."[25] Have you not found that to be true with seeing God? When you see and feel God, you just know.

Finding Purpose

When did you first begin to look for God?
Where have you seen God?
Who has led you to God?
How could you begin to see life from the right side?

Finding Scripture

In Lucy's struggles to convince her siblings that she had seen Aslan, we find parallels to Mary Magdalene's attempts to convince the disciples that Jesus had risen. Remember how Jesus appeared to Mary Magdalene and at first she did not know him? In relying only on her eyes, she did not recognize him. However, when he spoke her name, calling out "Mary," she turned and recognized him (John 20:17). Jesus then asked her to tell his apostles that she had seen him, like Aslan asked Lucy to tell her siblings that she had seen him.

Spiritual Blindness

Yet, some of the apostles did not recognize Jesus as quickly as Mary did. Luke tells of two apostles who met Jesus on the road to Emmaus. While they were "talking with each other about all these things that had happened,...Jesus himself came near and went with them" (Luke 24:14–15). Could you imagine walking and talking with Jesus? Apparently, they could not either. Because Luke (24:16) tells us, "their eyes were kept from recognizing him." This seems to be a theme common to scripture and Narnia. Some seeing requires more than physical eyesight. Lucy claimed that she just knew it was Aslan. She relied on an inner compass to recognize him.

Spiritual Seeing

Lewis allows us to find ourselves in Lucy and the apostles. He wants us to reflect on what prevents us from seeing God's presence around us. While conversing with the apostles on the way to Emmaus, Jesus hears that some of the apostles doubt whether he had really risen. Jesus reprimands them and calls them "foolish" because they are "slow of heart to believe." Then "beginning with Moses and all the prophets," he explains how the events had fulfilled the prophesies. Later, when Jesus breaks bread with them "their eyes were opened" and they realize that they had ignored their "hearts" which had been "burning within" while he had been speaking with them (Luke 24:13–35). Here we learn that seeing God requires a seeing with our hearts. We are also reassured that we can find God in the sacrament of the Eucharist, when we break bread with one another and share in Jesus's body. For after receiving the Eucharist do you not also feel your "heart burning within?" Jesus also uses scripture to help open the apostles' eyes to him. Don't we do that now—seeing God's presence at work in our lives through scripture, coming to know him, and how he works in our lives?

This message is repeated several times in the Gospels of Luke and John, just in case we miss it! Fortunately, God has patience with our slow learning and spiritual blindness. After the two disciples met him on the road to Emmaus, Luke tells us that Jesus appears again to the apostles. They are all startled at first and do not recognize him. In fact, Luke tells us "they were startled and terrified, and thought that they were seeing a ghost."

Again, Jesus refers to their hearts as a means for seeing him. In recognizing the fear that blinds them, Jesus questions, "Why are you frightened, and why do doubts arise in your hearts?" He then, like in the previous appearance, shares a meal with them and "opened their minds to understand the scriptures" (Luke 24:36–46). By placing these two accounts together, we understand that seeing God requires us to rely on our hearts, scripture, and sharing the Eucharist with other followers. To see God, we cannot rely on our eyes; we must develop an inner spiritual seeing.

John includes the story of the infamous doubting Thomas to remind us of our own failings in faith. Do you remember him? He was not present when Jesus appeared to the apostles. Because he was not present and did not see Jesus, he doubts their story. In fact he says, "Unless I see the mark of the nails in his hands, and put my finger in the mark of the nails and my hand in his side, I will not believe" (John 20:25). Do you not hear your own doubts here? Have you not also struggled at times with your faith, especially when life becomes especially burdensome? Where is God? Why does he not help me now?" Does this not also remind you of Susan and Trumpkin, the last ones to see Aslan? Jesus tells us "blessed are those who have not seen and yet have come to believe" (John 20:29). Here, Jesus addresses us. He knows that we will not be able to rely on our physical eyesight to believe in him.

Through the characters of Susan and Trumpkin, Lewis was displaying his own battles with spiritual blindness. In introducing these characters to us, Lewis helps us see ourselves. Through them, we see our failings and find ways to get back on track. Jesus shows us that we can turn to our faith community, scripture, and the Eucharist to feel the "burning" presence of him "within our hearts." Lucy also shows us that seeing God requires a trusting in our inner self and instincts. We need to listen to and follow what we know to be true, even when others do not see or believe. We need to listen to our hearts. Most importantly, we need to trust in our God, who will lead us and continue to reach out to us even when we are blind.

In *Letters to Children,* Lewis offers advice to his goddaughter, Sarah, on this matter as she is about to become confirmed and receive her first holy communion. He tells her:

> ...don't expect (I mean, don't *count on* and don't *demand*) that when you are confirmed, or when you make your first Communion, you will have all the *feelings* you would like to have. You may, of course: but you also may not. But don't worry if you don't get them. They aren't what matter. The things that are happening to you are quite real things whether you feel as you would wish or not, just as a meal will do a hungry person good even if he has a cold in the head which will spoil the taste.[26]

In this advice, Lewis realizes that even while he was blind, God was still at work leading him. In *Surprised by Joy,* he comically remarks, "a young man who wishes to remain a sound Atheist cannot be too careful of his reading. There are traps everywhere...God is, if I may say it, very unscrupulous."[27] Lewis reassures us here, as it is likely that most of us have been and will be lost again. He reminds us that God is real and is at work even when we cannot see him. In his letter to his goddaughter, Lewis also shows that the sacraments will keep us connected to God, even in those moments when we are following and receiving blindly.

> ## Suggested Scripture Reading and Reflections
>
> Read Luke 24 and John 20 to reflect on your own spiritual blindness.
>
> When have you, like the apostles, failed to see God's presence?
> What blinded you?
> How could you better use God's gifts of scripture, Eucharist, and your faith community to find God's presence?
> When have you seen God at work in your life?
> How did you know it was God?
> Susan and the apostles were blinded by fear; Thomas and Trumpkin were blinded by doubt; Lewis was blinded by a false intellect and desire for control. What seems to most often blind you to God's presence?
> How can you work to sharpen your spiritual seeing?

Returning to Days Past

Reflections on Lewis with Caspian

*I*n *Prince Caspian,* the children arrive in Narnia by a much different means than they do in *The Lion, the Witch and the Wardrobe.* While the first time they arrive by choosing to climb through a wardrobe, the second time they are literally pulled back by an unexplainable force. It is likely that Lewis shows us here that sometimes God speaks to us or calls out to us from far and distant places. Sometimes these places can come from our past.

In *Surprised by Joy,* Lewis describes a time where he felt one of these pulls that transported him back to the past. He refers to it as an event that was "in superabundance of mercy."[28] As Lewis waited at Leatherhead Station on a cool October evening while reading MacDonald's book, *Phantastes, a Faerie Romance for Men and Women,* he felt "the habitual imagery...lure [him] on without the perception of change."[29] He says, "It is as if I were carried sleeping across the frontier, or as if I had died in the old country and could never remember how I came alive in the new."[30] There he reconnected with loved ones of the past as "the sirens sounded like the voice of [his] mother or [his] nurse....It was as though the voices which had called to [him] from the world's end were now speaking at [his] side. It was with [him] in the room, or in [his] own body, or behind [him]."[31] Lewis named this "bright shadow," which lured him and took him on his travels, "Holiness." During this journey, his "imagination, was, in a certain sense, baptized."[32]

Personal Ponderings

Pulled Back to Remember

It is worth noting the similarities between Lewis's journey with Holiness on the platform of Leatherhead Station and the Pevensie children's journey that literally pulled them back to Narnia while they were also waiting at a train station. Sitting in front of the railway, bored with the idea of returning to school, they felt a strong pull. Before they knew it, they were back in Narnia. Gradually, the past spoke to them. As they found the gifts that Aslan had given to them—the potion, the horn, the bow and arrows, and the armor and swords—they remembered who they were, where they came from, and what they were called to do. Is this not also a type of baptism?

Haven't you also felt that pull back to the past? While in the midst of every day, mundane events, don't you hear your name whispered? Feel a tug? Suddenly you find yourself reliving a memory from years past. Like Lewis, Lucy, Edmund, Peter, and Susan, do you not "re-find gifts" that you have forgotten you have?

Trust in God

Last Advent, in the midst of cleaning, I was reminded of my grandmother. Finding herself a widow with seven children in the 1960s, she demonstrated a great sense of faith in God and remained a pillar of strength for the family. She lived each day with confidence, believing and knowing that God would take care of her and her children.

Through the grace and help of God, she raised all seven children into adulthood on her own. I am the oldest of my grandmother's youngest child, so I did not know her through most of her struggles. She lived a meager life and was fond of saying, "Trust in God. God will provide." Now, I often find these same words spilling from my mouth as I raise my own children.

A Visit from Christmas Past

The Christmas memory that tugged at me took me back to a Christmas Eve when I was ten years old. When gift time came, my grandmother handed each one of her grandchildren a neatly wrapped package that was under the tree.

"Here, Gina. This one is for you." She had such pride on her face as she handed it to me. I can still see the twinkle in her eye. I unwrapped my gift and found the usual crocheted purse—multicolored yarn woven around and hooked to an empty margarine container. Inside the purse sat a shiny penny. I took it out and felt the smoothness under my fingertips. I tossed it back nonchalantly into the purse. What can you buy with a penny? Remembering how proud she was to give me a gift still fills me with an enormous guilt. How could I be so selfish and unappreciative?

Forgotten Gifts

In my cleaning, I had bent down and found a penny. How often in cleaning, have you bent down and picked up a penny from the floor? While looking at it I noticed the words: "In God We Trust."

While my grandmother did not have the money to buy each of us an exciting new gift each Christmas, she spent the entire year weaving her love into purses that would carry the greatest gift she could ever give us. The lesson: "Trust in God." These words helped her through some of the toughest hardships and challenges that anyone could ever face.

When the world bombards and blinds me, I find myself bending over to pick up a penny that someone has carelessly dropped and left behind. I pick up the penny and think of my grandmother and her crocheted purses as I read: "In God We Trust." I put the penny in my pocket, smile, and whisper, "Thank you, Grandma."

Finding Purpose

When have you been pulled back to the past?

Who pulled you there?

What did you remember?

What spiritual gifts do you have that you have forgotten about?

Who gave you these gifts?

What will you do with the gifts you have been given?

Finding Scripture

In the account of the transfiguration, we see Peter, James, and John encounter Jesus on an extraordinary journey into the past where they meet Elijah and Moses. Luke tells us that while "[Jesus] was praying, the appearance of his face changed, and his clothes became dazzling white" (Luke 9:29). Then to their further astonishment and fear, Moses and Elijah appeared and began to converse with Jesus. Similar to Lewis, the Pevensie children, and myself, the apostles are pulled into an almost dreamlike reality where they are reunited with people from the past—people who will teach them what they need to know.

Just as Lewis heard the voices of his mother and nurse, the Pevensies talked again with and learned from Aslan, and I was retaught the lesson of my grandmother, the apostles hear the booming voice of God from a cloud proclaiming, "This is my Son, my Chosen; listen to him!" (Luke 9:35). While Jesus instructs them not to tell of the events until after his death, they later realize as we do now that Moses's presence represented the Old Testament law, and Elijah's presence represented the prophets. Moses and Elijah signified that the prophecies and laws of the past were about to be fulfilled. Jesus was about to endure an exodus from Jerusalem to free us from sin and allow us to one day reunite with him in God's paradise, paralleling Moses' exodus from Egypt that freed the Israelites and led them into the promised land. Jesus tells the apostles and us that Elijah came as predicted in John the Baptist. He was not recognized and was put to death, just as Jesus the Son of God will be. The booming voice of God reaffirmed this by identifying Jesus, for the second time, as the Messiah—the Son of God.

In taking the apostles and us on the mountain to meet Moses, Elijah, and to see him transfigured, Jesus pulls us into the past. He gets his apostles' attention in an extraordinary way, so that he can deliver an important message to them. To requote Lewis's description of his own experience, on the mountaintop the apostles encountered the "superabundance of mercy" and met "holiness" in its truest form. Sometimes we need to be pulled out of our daily routines to hear the voice of God.

Suggested Scripture Reading and Reflections

Read the three accounts of the transfiguration (Matt 17:1–6; Mark 9:1–8; Luke 9:28–36) and reflect on how Jesus uses the extraordinary to speak to and teach his apostles.

Why do you think Jesus only took Peter, James, and John with him?

When has God singled you out to deliver a message?

Why do you think you were chosen?

What extraordinary ways has God used to speak to you?

What did you learn in the experience?

Why do you think the apostles were frightened?

Would you have been?

Jesus reassured them so that fear would not keep them from opening themselves up to the experience. How has Jesus reassured you in times of fear?

All of these stories have a theme of travel and journey. What journey are you currently traveling?

How is it extraordinary?

How are you overcoming the challenges and fears?

What are you learning?

Growing Out of Imagination

Reflections on Lewis with Caspian

*L*ewis reunites with his childhood imagination in Narnia. The beginning pages of *Surprised by Joy* show us how as a youth he "was living almost entirely in imagination" and that in looking back, "the imaginative experience of those years" seemed "more important than anything else."[33] Later in life, the imaginative experiences where he met "Joy" led him back to his faith. However, he distinguishes this type of imagination from the "world of reverie, daydream, wish fulfilling fantasy"[34] and tells us that while he did partake in those experiences, those experiences were not the important ones. Rather, it was the imaginative experiences of the "third sense, and the highest sense of all"[35] that were "in another dimension" and "in a sense the central story of his life."[36] For Lewis, these experiences were triggered by the intersection of nature and literature. At that intersection, he found the dimension of God. He describes these experiences as leaving one with a sense of longing that he calls "Joy" and says that it "is itself more desirable than any other satisfaction" and that "anyone who has experienced it will want it again."[37]

In his Narnia series, Lewis invites us into that experience. By combining nature and literature, he invites us into the dimension of the divine where we come to know Jesus as a lion. In this realm, children and adults come together to experience the imagination that Lewis described as a longing. In Narnia, our inner senses are reawakened and sharpened in a way that will lead us back to our God. Our meeting of Aslan helps us to understand better the complex book of Revelation when the "Lion of the tribe of Judah" triumphs over death so that the "scroll and its seven seals" can be opened (Rev 5:5). The lion of Narnia helps us to see Jesus as the lion of Judah who saves us from death. Lewis attests to this in a letter addressed to Carol. He tells her that he found the name Aslan "in the notes to Lane's *Arabian Nights:* it is the Turkish for lion…and of course I meant the Lion of Judah."[38]

Interestingly, adults were concerned about children's adoration of the lion of Narnia. In a letter to Mrs. K, we get a glimpse of this concern, when the mother expresses her fear that her son loves Aslan more than he loves Jesus. Lewis reassures her by explaining that the very qualities that attract her son to Aslan are the same traits of Jesus. He tells her:

> Nevertheless, Laurence cannot *really* love Alsan more than Jesus, even if he feels that's what he is doing. For the things he loves Aslan for doing or saying are simply the things Jesus really did and said. So that when Laurence thinks he is loving Aslan, he is really loving Jesus: and perhaps loving him even more than he ever did before.[39]

Clearly, this letter shows our adult tendencies to lose sight of our childlike innocence. Caught up in intellectual issues, Mrs. K fears the very experience that may lead her son to Jesus. Laurence, obviously, is oblivious to the whole issue and is caught up in loving Aslan. Lewis eloquently explains that this will grow to become a love for Jesus. Fortunately, God addresses these fears through Lewis and shows Mrs. K that perhaps her child is wiser in this issue than she is.

Lewis's brother, Warren, also gives credence to the spiritual phenomenon of Narnia in his introduction of *Letters to Children.* He tells us that many of the letters children wrote to Lewis "centered on the Narnian books, the spiritual reality within these stories," and "not surprisingly, these were the same topics Lewis was often asked to address by his adult readers."[40] Even more convincing is a letter from an eleven-year-old girl named Hila who writes about "an indefinable stirring and longing"[41] that she felt while reading Narnia. In writing Narnia, Lewis was granted the gift of creating an experience that may re-awaken our own childlike imagination.

Never Coming Back

Many of us felt our hearts ache in sorrow for Peter and Susan when Peter shared with Edmund and Lucy what Aslan had told him. Peter and Susan would "not [be] coming back to Narnia." Edmund and Lucy also cried in dismay, "Never?"[42]

How could Aslan be so unfair? Surely, Peter and Susan should be able to return to Narnia. They deserved it as much as Lucy and Edmund. Why would Peter and Susan not be coming back? Aslan wouldn't keep Peter and Susan out of Narnia. I am guessing that Aslan knew Peter and Susan would forget how to return. They would grow too old in their thinking to find it. Is not that also true of ourselves? Haven't we also forgotten how to find Narnia? Don't we also act as though we have outgrown it?

In *Letters to Children,* Lewis responds to a young boy named Martin about Susan's quandary and gives us some insight into our struggles with remaining childlike. He tells us:

> The books do not tell us what happened to Susan. She is left alive in this world at the end, having by then turned into a rather silly, conceited young woman. However, there is plenty of time for her to mend, and perhaps she will get to Aslan's country in the end—in her own way. I think that whatever she had seen in Narnia she *could* (if she was the sort that wanted to) persuade herself, as she grew up, that it was "all nonsense."[43]

Lewis seems to be speaking about his struggles here as well as speaking to all of us. As adults, don't we also become quite conceited and think of ourselves as sophisticated and intelligent? We lose touch with the innocence that allowed us to imagine, and some of us become lost as we even convince ourselves at times that matters of faith are "all nonsense."

Lewis experienced this as he spent many years as an atheist. Ironically, in *Surprised by Joy,* he tells us how God later used the words of "the hardest boiled of all atheists"[44] to bring him back from his "deep-seated hatred of authority," "monstrous individualism," and "lawlessness"[45] that had stamped out his faith in adulthood. Lewis tells us "on the other side of the fire" the atheist "remarked that the evidence for the historicity of the Gospels was really surprisingly good."[46] He explains that this "had a shattering impact"[47] and brought a "repercussion on the imaginative level."[48] In deciding to "open the door...to unbuckle, to loosen the rein,"[49] he "felt as if [he] were a man of snow at long last beginning to melt."[50] In his melting, one cannot help but think of the White Witch's snow kingdom melting and giving way to spring. In Narnia, Lewis found how to be a child again.

Personal Ponderings

To Be a Child Again

Many children enjoy listening to stories about their parents' childhood. In the midst of our busy adult life, we tend to forget about our childhood days. Sometimes it takes a while to recall a story to tell them, but when they begin telling us about their own adventures, a secret entrance opens up, and we find ourselves climbing through a window into our own childhood. "That reminds me of a day when..." And the adventure begins as we remember roller skating backward, riding a bike down the big hill with no hands, building sand castles, finding a tree house, and exploring nature.

Do You Hear What I Hear?

My backyard bordered a cornfield, and I was convinced that Indians had once lived there. At least once a week, I led my neighborhood friends to search the tall weeds outside the cornfield to find "Indian stuff." Mostly, we found what we called Indian rocks— smooth rocks with a beige ring around a purple center.

After our search, we would return to our Indian hut, which consisted of a matted down area in the middle of the tall weeds. There we would close our eyes and try to hear the beating of Indian drums. I was sure that I had heard them once.

"Do you hear that?" I whispered with my eyes still closed.

"Hear what?" they responded.

"Shh. Listen. I hear drums," I whispered again.

Everyone became very quiet.

"I don't hear anything," one of them retorted. "You are just making it up."

"No. Listen. It is coming closer. Look, the weeds are even starting to move. The Indians are coming."

They opened their eyes and watched as the weeds behind us began to sway back and forth. That was all it took. Within seconds, they all stood up and ran home in fright.

Rather perturbed, I yelled, "You scared them away. The drums are gone."

Sometimes I wish I could be that little girl again. The girl who listened for Indian drums and sat in matted down weeds. Now I will not go near long weeds—there could be snakes! The cell phone, fax machine, washing machine, e-mail, and grading of papers block out any distant sounds of my past—the drums are gone.

Could this be what Aslan meant when he told Peter that he and Susan were getting too old to return to Narnia? Had Aslan known that Peter and Susan would lose the ability to hear "the drums" like I have?

Finding Purpose

What is one of your favorite childhood adventures?
What did you imagine as a child?
How could you become more like a little child?

Finding Scripture

Like Little Children

Jesus reminds us "unless you change and become like children, you will never enter the kingdom of heaven" (Matt 18:3). Imagine that—never enter the kingdom of heaven. Although there are many interpretations of this Bible verse, Jesus appears to be reminding us to hold on to our ability to imagine.

As we get older, we only look at what is tangible and identified with our senses, but children are different. They spend most of their day imagining. They believe in what they cannot see. This takes a type of humbling—to believe that other powers and forces are present and greater than you. It requires that we trust in a God who we cannot see with physical eyesight. Jesus tells us, "Whoever becomes humble like this child is the greatest in the kingdom of heaven" (Matt 18:4). He clearly states that we must retain our childlike innocence to enter God's kingdom. Likewise, we must remember to value the wisdom of children.

For Jesus also tells us, "Whoever welcomes one such child in my name welcomes me" (Matt 18:5).

Children naturally know that imagining does not rely on our senses. It requires that we break free from the every day way of life. It makes us let go of fact and reality. It forces us to jump into a realm of feeling—sit in matted down weeds listening for distant drums. In this realm, we tap into what might be and learn to trust and believe in what we cannot see and touch. We learn to believe in what we feel with our heart and soul. This is the realm where we find God. No wonder, Jesus tells us we will "never enter the kingdom of heaven" unless we become like little children. We will not enter it because we will not find it. We will not be able to imagine it. In this passage, Jesus reminds us to value and listen to his little ones.

Our children and the Pevensie children help us to remember what it means to be a little child. Without them and their unique insights that challenge adults who are preoccupied in their own world of living, we may never find God's kingdom.

Suggested Scripture Reading and Reflections

Read Matthew 18:1–5 and reflect on the qualities of children. Think about how Jesus values them as the "greatest" in his kingdom.

What imaginary activities did you enjoy as a child?
When has a child helped you re-find that childlike innocence?
What did you learn in that experience?
How can you let go of the adultlike thinking that causes us to lose touch with our faith?

The Myth of Power

Reflections on Lewis with Caspian

*I*n reading Lewis's letters to Arthur Greeves, Lewis's humanness seems evident. He was not always a devoted Christian and struggled with matters of faith. There is something confessional and deeply personal about letter writing. Lewis tells Greeves that letters should speak of our "doings, readings, thinkings."[51] Following his own advice, his letters to Greeves record his doings, readings, thinkings that offer an understanding of what led him astray.

Lewis personified many of the emotions that can lead us astray in the character of Nikabrik—fear, anger, and desire for control and power. We also see his own struggles with these emotions weave through his letter "arguing" and theological discussions. One of the most telling arguments begins with Lewis's use of the word *exaltation*. Whereas Lewis uses the word to refer a dream-like state, Greeves immediately comments on its religious connotations. Lewis becomes frustrated with this connection and attempts "to explain again" how he intended the word to be read. From this discussion, a lengthy conversation on Christianity unfolds where Lewis shares that he "believe[s] in no religion."[52]

In the letters he argues there is "absolutely no proof" and finds "all religions" to be "merely man's own invention" to explain all the "terrible things he didn't understand." Perhaps we find insight into Lewis's reasoning here as he only notes the "terrible" things and then lists "thunder, pestilence, snakes," as examples. Furthermore, he continues to say that man animated these fearful things with "evil spirits trying to torture him." He then writes that these spirits were eventually elevated to gods who man then pretended "were good as well as powerful."[53]

In this discussion with Greeves, Lewis really masks his own reasoning and fears by talking about what "primitive man found himself surrounded by."[54] Here we see that Lewis's doubts were really fears. He perceives man and himself at odds with nature. Creation is scary and unpleasant. Perhaps this has roots in his mother's early death. God was controlling, unfair, and to be feared.

He chooses to see himself outside of religion, where he can determine his own "morals," which he says, "we owe to our own manhood and dignity and not to any imagined god or gods."[55] Clearly, we see Lewis's desire to be in control here. This becomes even more apparent as he refuses "to go back to the bondage of believing."[56] At this stage of his life, Lewis saw Christianity as painful and infringing. His fear and desire for control gave birth to doubt, which in turn led to "occasional fits of depression."[57] Later in *Surprised by Joy* when Lewis reflects on his dark travels to atheism, he personally calls attention to his "pessimism" and connects it to his desire to control and be free from interruptions.[58] He says:

> I was at this time living, like so many Atheists or Antitheists, in a whirl of contradictions. I maintained that God did not exist. I was also very angry with God for not existing. I was equally angry with him for creating a world....I now see that my view was closely connected with a certain lopsidedness of temperament. I had always been more violent in my negative than in my positive demands. Thus, in personal relations, I could forgive much neglect more easily than the least degree of what I regarded as interference.[59]

In summary, Lewis did not want to believe in a God who he negatively perceived as uncaring, cruel, and unnecessarily infringing. His pessimistic outlook led to fear, anger, and a loss of faith and hope.

Desperate Doubts

Nikabrik personifies this dark side of Lewis, a side that we do not like to see, especially in ourselves. Nikabrik unmasks the same fears, angers, and doubts that plagued Lewis through much of his life. Nikabrik may have also given Lewis the symbolic opportunity to look at and bury his own character.

We see this in chapter 12, when Nikabrik's reasoning sounds similar to young Lewis's arguments to Greeves: "Either Aslan is dead, or he is not on our side." Then in desperation, he proclaims: "We want a power that will be on our side."[60] Like the younger atheist Lewis who was angry with a god who he pessimistically viewed as uncaring, Nikabrik views Aslan in much the same way.

At first, Nikabrik's words stir horror. With Edmund and Caspian, we gasp and wonder how Nikabrik could say such evil things. Yet upon deeper reflection, do you not secretly remember the times when you doubted in the midst of hopelessness and despair? Have you not wondered where God was and why he was not coming to your rescue? Have you not at least temporarily wondered about a greater power, the power that was causing pain and suffering in this life? Have you not at times asked, "Where is God?" Why is he not stopping this pain, this evil? Is God really more powerful than Satan?

Personal Ponderings

The Trained Eye

Sometimes a tragic situation teaches us the importance of how to live our lives. The Pennsylvania schoolhouse shooting involving young Amish girls is an example. A man, Charles

Roberts, fighting demons from his past left suicide notes for his family, took his children to the bus stop, and then entered a one-room schoolhouse where he opened fire on the Amish girls. He then killed himself. A reporter indicated that Roberts had been angry with God.

Many wonder and vocalize the questions in the midst of such a tragedy: "How could God let this happen? Why didn't God stop him?" A feeble response that "God works in strange ways sometimes" is an inadequate explanation.

As the story continued to unfold, the focus began to change. The Amish community did not give way to fear and despair. They reached out to the family of the killer in love and forgiveness. They did not scream out to God in anger and like Nikabrik ask for a greater power to be on their side. They never felt that God abandoned them. They wisely understood that nothing was really lost. We do not live for this life. Death is not the end. To quote Amish researcher Gertrude Huntington, the Amish "don't balance the hurt with hate."[61] They wisely balance hate with love.

Rather than focusing on the hate of the killer, we admiringly saw God's love and goodness reaching out to the killer's family through the Amish community. This tragedy became an opportunity for a religious group of people to rejoice in the power of God and the power of love.

Stories of Faith: The Power of Love

The Amish used their tragedy to help us understand the power of love. They knew that they could undo the evil that hate unleashed upon them by loving the family of their perpetrator. They rose above death and hate. If we read our newspapers and watched the news with the same eyes we read scripture, this would not surprise us. Like Badger, we would see through the evil and proclaim amidst violence, hate, death and doubt, "But they also say that he came to life again."[62] We would focus on the love that always emerges from tragedy. Good always prevails. We just need to look for it.

When hate sent planes of fear and death on September 11, firefighters rose with love and courage. When the eye of faith looks back on that day, it sees the firefighters unselfishly rushing into burning towers. We remember them proudly holding our country's flag showing that hate would not prevail. We remember the prayer vigils and hands folded to our God.

Likewise, when we remember the school shootings in Columbine, Colorado, we see a young girl facing a gun being asked, "Do you believe in God?" and we hear her confidently respond, "Yes, I do" before she falls to the ground. In those attacks of hate, love triumphed and faith grew stronger. God won, not Satan. However, we must look through different eyes to see this. We must realize that death is not the end.

This is what I must tell others, my children, and myself when they ask me, "Where is God? Why do our loved ones die? Why does the bad guy always seem to win?" As Trufflehunter responded to Nikabrik, we must respond with confidence and help them see and hear stories of faith where love always wins over hate.

Finding Purpose

When have you sounded and acted like Nikabrik?

How can you train yourself to look for good?

When have you seen love triumph over hate?

How has Jesus's triumph over sin and death changed your life?

Finding Scripture

We doubt because we are human. However, in the Gospels, we find hope and understanding when we realize that God entered our world in the person of Jesus to bring an end to our suffering. He did not abandon us, but rather defeated Satan and evil in the resurrection. Satan foolishly believed that death would erase our faith in a higher being. As promised, Jesus rose from death, forgave his apostles and us for fearing and doubting in the midst of death and turmoil, and freed us from sin and death forever. God defeated Satan similar to how Aslan defeated the White Witch.

Yet, our preoccupation with this world and our negative outlook often cause us to forget this message. Like Nikabrik and Lewis, we easily fall prey to doubt and fear. Most often, we doubt and fear in times of death, violence, and confusion.

The Gospel of John tells us that Jesus visited his disciples after his resurrection. He found their doors locked out of fear for the Jews. In the midst of death and turmoil, they also turned to fear. However, Jesus eased their fears by showing them his wounds and saying, "Peace be with you." He also "breathed on them" as Aslan breathed on the Pevensie children and told them to "receive the Holy Spirit." Thomas, not with them at the time, did not believe the disciples recounting of the experience. He only believed later when Jesus allowed him to touch his wounds and says to Thomas and us, "Do not doubt, but believe" (John 20:19–28).

The disciples, especially Thomas, mirror Lewis and all of us. They doubt in times of chaos and fear. Jesus eases their fears with visible reminders and the presence of the Holy Spirit. Does he not do the same for us? When we are in our deepest of doubts, does he not send the right person or some sign to redirect our thoughts and seeing? Do we not in those times come face to face with the Holy Spirit?

In times of doubt and fear, many often look to the book of Revelation for answers. They want a visible sign of when the world will end. Although it does speak of the end times, reading it for predicting an exact date often leads faithful followers into despair and disbelief. However, reading it in its apocalyptic style brings us hope in times of doubt.

As noted in the reading guide of *The Catholic Study Bible,* the "Apocalyptic defends God's justice." While the events in the books seem "to be under the control of evil people or even satanic powers…just when things become humanly impossible on earth, God will intervene (as through a Messiah) to save his own, and inaugurate the 'kingdom of God.'"[63] Keeping this in mind, the book of Revelation offers us hope and reminds us that even in the darkest and scariest times, God will intervene and rescue his faithful.

My sense is that Lewis intentionally leads us to the book of Revelation through the Lion. As mentioned earlier in this section, he intended Aslan the lion to represent the Lion of the tribe of Judah. In Revelation, John tells us that in this vision he was told not to weep because "the Lion of the tribe of Judah, the Root of David, has conquered" (Rev 5:5). A hymn is then sung to the lion by the twenty-four elders speaking of the lion's worthiness to "take the scroll and to open its seals" because it was "slaughtered" and "by [its] blood [it] ransomed…saints from every tribe and language and people and nation…and they will reign on earth" (Rev 5:5–14). Does this scene in Revelation not remind you of a scene from Narnia?

Lewis's use of the symbolic imagery of the lion helps to better enter into and understand the complex and symbolic world of revelation. He leads us here to give us hope. By falling in love with Aslan and yearning for the land of Narnia, we are led to the apocalyptic world of revelation that is intended to give us hope.

It reminds us that pain and evil will not reign forever. Jesus died for us, and the evil of this world will come to an end. God will prevail, and we will rejoice in God's kingdom.

Suggested Scripture Reading and Reflections

Read chapter 20 of John and reflect on it in light of your experience of doubting.

When have you found yourself doubting?

What emotions lead you to doubt?

In *Surprised by Joy*, Lewis describes how key figures in his life and literature greatly affected his spiritual journey both positively and negatively. What and who seems to most influence your faith journey?

Consider a time when your thinking was turned around. When were you able to see a negative experience more positively?

What helped you to re-see the experience?

When have you felt or seen the presence of God at work in your life?

How did it ease your fears and doubts?

Read chapters 4 and 5 from the book of Revelation by reflecting on the images and symbols described.

What emotions do they stir?

How are they similar to or different from the feelings you have about Narnia?

How might these chapters offer you hope?

Being Called

Reflections on Lewis with Caspian

*N*ot long after Lewis accepted that there was a God, he felt himself as "a man of snow at long last beginning to melt," and found himself presented with a "real terror." He could no longer just continue "to play at philosophy." He tells us:

> As the dry bones shook and came together in that dreadful valley of Ezekiel's, son now a philosophical theorem, cerebrally entertained, began to stir and heave and throw off its gravecloths, and stood upright and became a living presence.[64]

In this encounter, Lewis came face to face with a God who demanded "total surrender, the absolute leap in the dark." Literally and symbolically, this encounter came at night while he was "alone in that room in Magdalen." There he found the "unrelenting approach of Him whom [he] so earnestly desired not to meet" because he did not want to be "interfered with" and he did not want to be "lead into anything intolerably painful." Yet, there in the middle of the night God found him and demanded "all." No longer able to deny God's call, he "admitted God was God, and knelt and prayed." Finding divine mercy in God's acceptance of his "reluctant" surrender, Lewis describes "the hardness of God is kinder than the softness of men, and his compulsion is our liberation."[65]

In the Still of the Night

Certainly Lewis did not want to be awoken from his spiritual slumber. On the simplest of levels, none of us likes to be woken from our sleep. Even when we know someone else depends on us, it is very hard. As parents who have been awakened to feed crying babies, explain away nightmares, and comfort sick children, many of us can relate to Lewis's reluctance not to be "interfered with." We want to be in control and remain removed from inconvenience and pain.

In *Prince Caspian,* Lewis portrays this viewpoint with Caspian's sleepiness and reluctance to be pulled from his slumber by Doctor Cornelius. Even though adventure is upon him and he longs to hear more of Doctor Cornelius's stories, he would rather sleep. However, Doctor Cornelius persists and takes him out of the comfort of his safe bed. In the chill of the evening, we shiver with Caspian and listen with droopy eyes as Doctor Cornelius finishes his story of Old Narnia and tells Caspian of how he can help make up for the mistakes of past Telmarines. He calls Caspian to action. He presents him with a mission.

Personal Ponderings

Hearing God's Call

God speaks to us in many ways throughout the day. Sometimes his voice is hard to hear through all the distractions. As Lewis and Caspian demonstrate, the world has a way of lulling us into a spiritual slumber. Sometimes we cannot even decipher God's voice from all of the other voices bombarding us. "Is that really you, God?" Like Lewis and Caspian, the biggest challenge is overcoming ourselves. We try to reason that what God has told us does not make sense or that we have misheard the message.

A few years ago, like Lewis and Caspian, I received one of God's messages in the middle of the night. For some reason, I awoke with an urgency to tell my mother that her father loved her and was proud of her. This came out of nowhere, and it was especially unsettling for me because I had never met my grandfather. He had died when my mother was eleven years old.

I wanted to shake it off and tried to remember what shows that I had watched and articles I had recently read. Did any of them mention death, fathers, and messages from the grave? There was no logical explanation. It seemed to be one of those many weird dreams I too often have and went back to sleep.

In the morning, the message still haunted me, and there was such urgency to it. I did not relish bringing up painful memories for my mother. How could I give her such a cryptic message, one that I did not even understand?

What Does It Mean?

The urgency to share this message with my mother went on for months and would not go away. It just kept resurfacing and nagging at me. Deep down I knew that it was not going away.

At Mass, I prayerfully took it to God. What does this mean? Is this you speaking to me? Do you really want me to deliver this message to my mom? A warm peace filled me, and I knew that God wanted the message delivered. I prayed for courage.

After Mass, my husband and I had breakfast with my parents; mom and I went out on the deck. We sat on the benches drinking coffee as the spring breeze blew through our hair. I took a deep breath and began.

"Mom, I got this weird message a few months ago that I think I am supposed to give you. I haven't said anything about it because it is...well, kind of odd."

Mom just looked and me and kind of laughed nervously. She had that look of "now what." Having nine children, she never knew what to expect.

43

"Well, I don't know why, but I think I am supposed to tell you…" I braced myself for the reaction. "Your dad loves you and is proud of you." I breathed a sigh of relief; finally, it was out.

My mother looked kind of shaken, as I thought to myself that I should not have said anything. She responded quietly: "Really. I have been praying for that answer for a few months now. I have been praying about my dad and his death, trying to heal. That message answers my prayers. Thank you."

A sense of relief came over her. She hugged me and thanked me again for sharing it. I was shocked and somewhat ashamed. Why did God deliver this through me? Why hadn't I told her sooner?

Understanding God

As humans, we may never fully understand God and what God asks of us while we are here on earth. God works in ways different from our own. Like Lewis eloquently said, "God is God." But he does work through us. Like Lewis and Caspian, we need to be willing to wake from our slumber to listen and have the courage and faith to act.

Finding Purpose

When has God called you and delivered a message?
What is God calling you to do?
Why is it so hard to hear God's voice?
When have you been spiritually asleep?

Finding Scripture

How many of God's people have been called from their slumber to hear God's voice and receive a message? How often does God speak through dreams? Samuel particularly comes to mind (1 Sam 3:1–18). Remember how, as a young boy, Samuel was called from his sleep several times before he realized it was God speaking to him? He falsely recognizes the voice as that of Eli. When he finally realizes it is God and says, "Speak, LORD, for your servant is listening" (1 Sam 3:9), he hears a frightful message that he does not want to deliver to Eli. As Lewis shares of his own calling and demonstrates with the character of Caspian, being called may be frightening—and it often requires us to leave the comfort of our slumber and encounter pain.

Suggested Scripture Reading and Reflections

Read 1 Samuel 3:1–18 and reflect on your own calling by God.

What kept Samuel from recognizing God?

When have you felt like Samuel?

Lewis found "God's compulsion is our liberation." Was this true for Samuel?

Is it true for you?

Getting Lost

Reflections on Lewis with Caspian

We all find ourselves lost at times. In a letter to Greeves, Lewis tells of one such time where he wandered for hours, even "with the aid of a map." He captures the real experience of "expecting to reach the place" only to find yourself "in a place where" you "had been an hour before."[66] This experience spoke strongly enough to Lewis that he wrote about it to Greeves.

Knowing that others also go through times of being lost, he shared this experience through the characters in *Prince Caspian.* However, in *Prince Caspian,* he adds another symbolic dimension, the experience of being spiritually lost. In this scene, Lewis sees himself in Peter, who takes responsibility for leading the others astray.

Alone in the Dark

When Peter admits in chapter 9 that they are lost and says, "It's all my fault for coming this way," we can feel his agony. Anyone who has ever been lost knows how tough it is to admit that you took a wrong turn. It is even more dreadful when you find yourself wondering and ranting like Trumpkin, "What chance have we of finding our way back?" The characters wander around in Narnia for hours not knowing where they are headed.[67]

Yet, while Lewis knows the dread of being both physically and spiritually lost, he also knows the joy of finding himself back. Thus, he allows us to get lost with the characters so that we can remember our own experiences of being lost. He wants us to reflect on both the physical and spiritual turmoil of wandering astray. Yet, he also wants us to remember that feeling of hope that comes when you find yourself where "trees tower up on rising ground, and every road from it is at once swallowed up in them. You might walk within a few feet of it and suspect nothing, unless you saw the smoke rising up...."[68] If we look for the "rising smoke" or listen to those who can see like Lucy, we will find our way back.

Personal Ponderings

Rising Smoke

The following story, as it was told to me, reminds me of Lewis's experience. It also shows us how we must keep our eyes open in order to find our way back. A young boy, Adam, had gone with his grandfather, uncle, and two cousins to spend the night outdoors on his grandfather's farm. This experience became an unexpected wilderness survival test. After sitting around the campfire telling stories and listening to the howls of coyotes, his grandfather went off to his tent to sleep. However, his uncle had other plans. He decided to take the boys for a midnight hike by the light of the moon.

The four of them tromped through the woods, admired the moon, pointed out hooting owls, and listened to howling coyotes. But as they reached the outer boundaries of the cow pasture, the uncle decided to ditch them by slipping off into the trees out of sight to see if they could find their way back to the campsite.

Adam's cousin Aaron was the first to complain about his father ditching them. In fact, like Trumpkin, he began to flip out.

"Oh, no. What are we going to do? I can't even see where I am going. It is too dark," Aaron wailed. Andrew, Aaron's brother and the oldest of the three, tried to keep his cool, but he was also afraid. Since he grew up in the Philippines, Iowa farms and forests were unfamiliar to him.

Adam was not surprised his uncle had ditched him. In fact, he had somewhat predicted it earlier. He had been making mental markings in his head about how to find his way back, just in case. Looking in the sky behind them, the moon revealed the smoke from their campfire.

Aaron continued to groan as he stepped into a hidden hole in the ground. "Ouch. I twisted my ankle. We will never find our way back!" A coyote howled in the distance, and Aaron dropped to the ground and began to crawl. "I am staying down here so the coyotes can't see me," he informed the others.

Andrew was a little shaken, but certainly not as worried as Aaron. "Aaron, the coyotes are too far away to see you. Get up!" Andrew reasoned as he walked into an unseen tree and yelped in pain. Adam kept walking toward the fire, listening and grinning at his cousins' misfortunes. This was the best humor of the night.

Aaron continued to crawl on the ground, sometimes falling into holes. Andrew ignored him and followed behind Adam. After a few minutes, Aaron let out a loud scream. "There are crickets jumping around in my hair. Help me!" Adam turned around and began to giggle. "It isn't funny, Adam!"

Aaron retorted with his hands feeling around in his hair and swatting in the air. Andrew reached down and pulled Aaron from the ground. "You are only falling in holes down there. Get up."

Adam, deciding the fun had gone on long enough, pointed at the rising smoke from the campfire. "We are not really lost. See the smoke? That is our campsite. We just need to walk toward it. Follow me." The three boys walked the rest of the way in silence toward the campsite.

Finding Our Way Back

Similar to the story of Peter, the three boys were lost in the dark. Like Adam, the Pevensie children were in familiar territory. They had been in Narnia before. Lucy sees Aslan pointing out the correct path to take, but the older children do not listen nor believe her. They remain lost much longer and end up taking a more difficult path. What if Aaron and Andrew had not followed Adam? They may have spent the night in the woods.

Both stories remind me of how we can become spiritually lost. We wander off in the darkness and need to find our way back. If we are in a familiar environment, it is easier to find our way. Sometimes we need a guide, someone to point us back in the right direction. We also need to know that we have truly found the right path. In commenting on his own journey back to faith, Lewis also notes the importance of a guide who sees the signpost. However, he also helps us distinguish when we have truly found the right path:

> When we are lost in the woods the sight of a signpost is a great matter. He who first sees it cries, "Look!" The whole party gathers round and stares. But when we have found the road and are passing signposts every few miles, we shall not stop and stare. They will encourage us and we shall be grateful to the authority that set them up.[69]

The key is to recognize the signposts, and to do this God gives us spiritual eyesight so that we will know when we are truly following on the path to him.

Finding Purpose

When have you been lost?
How did you feel?
When have you been spiritually lost?
How did you find your way back?
Who was your guide?

Finding Scripture

In chapter 9 of the Acts of the Apostles, we find Saul as an example of one who emerged from spiritual and physical darkness. After Jesus's death and resurrection, Saul led many persecutions against Jesus's disciples. He went about the streets looking for Jesus's followers, either murdering them or taking them back in chains to the high priests.

However, God did not give up on Saul. He admired his charisma and dedication. Knowing that Saul was lost and that his talents might be redirected for good, God found Saul while he was traveling to Damascus. Appearing in a great and startling light, God made Saul fall to the ground and called out to him: "Saul, Saul, why do you persecute me?" (Acts 9:4). Startled but not fully ready to find his way out of spiritual darkness, God placed Saul in total physical darkness to get his attention. Saul could not see for three days.

Yet, as God does for all of us if we want to see, he sent Ananias to guide Saul out of his darkness. Ananias was afraid to seek out Saul because of his past crimes against the disciples, but he trusted that God would keep him safe. Finding the blind Saul as God told him he would, Ananias restored Saul's sight and baptized him. Saul recognized Ananias as a guide and found his way out of darkness.

Suggested Scripture Reading and Reflections

Read Acts 9:1–22 and pay attention to the various details described in this conversion story.

Saul mistakenly believed he was doing what was right. He did not even know he was lost. When have your actions been misguided?

When and how did God redirect you?

When have you experienced spiritual darkness?

How did you find your way out?

Ananias was afraid of what God asked him to do, but he
trusted God. Because of his trust, he was able to lead
Saul out of his darkness.

When have you been like Ananias and helped someone find
his or her way out of spiritual darkness?

How did it feel?

Closed Doors

Reflections on Lewis with Caspian

*A*lthough there are times we shy away way from serving and
acting on our faith, there are also times that we believe we should
carry out some of God's tasks. Yet, sometimes it confusingly creates a spiritual quandary for us. When we do not feel confident
to perform a task, we find ourselves asked to serve. When we are
eager, ready, and willing, we find ourselves overlooked. This lesson appears in chapter 15 of *Prince Caspian*.

Aslan asks Prince Caspian if he feels sufficient "to take up
the Kingship of Narnia" and Caspian responds, "I—I don't think
I do, Sir. I am only a kid." Aslan responds, "Good. If you had felt
yourself sufficient, it would have been proof that you were not."[70]

Lewis contrasts this later in the chapter when Reepicheep
steps forward valiantly in front of the door in the air and offers
his services to Aslan by saying, "If my example can be of any service, Aslan, I will take eleven mice through that arch at your bid-

ding without a moment's delay." Aslan turns down Reepicheep's offer and closes the door to him: "Nay, little one."[71]

Is this not how it is with God? Sometimes we are called to act when we feel incapable, and yet other times, when we proudly and valiantly offer our gifts like Reepicheep, God turns us down and closes a door. The closed-door experiences are the most confusing and hard to handle. Like Reepicheep, many tend to be overly eager to serve.

Lewis also found this frustrating as he applied and waited for a position for many years at Oxford. In a letter written on October 28, 1922, Lewis writes to his father that he is "quite sure that an academic or literary career is the only one" in which he will find success. He dedicated many years to academic study at his father's expense and his own frequent worries about money and anxiety. His journal entries from 1923 show his anxiety and frustration as he continues to find himself waiting for a fellowship that never seems to appear. On February 9 he "was attacked by a series of gloomy thoughts about professional and literary failure"; on February 13 he again writes of being "haunted by fears for the future, as whether [he] will ever get a job, and whether [he] shall ever be able to write good poetry." In June these fears still plague him as he says that he was "in such a rage against poverty and fear and all the infernal net [he] seemed to be in that [he] went out and mowed the lawn and cursed all the gods for half an hour."[72]

Many of us can humorously relate to Lewis's ranting since we see and hear ourselves. Have you not also experienced this?—doubts, frustration, and anxiety about money and the future? Do you wonder why doors continue to close? Yet have you not later found that God knew what he was doing? Isn't his timing always perfect?

Two years later on May 26, 1925, Lewis finally writes proudly to his father of his election to a fellowship at Magdalen. He thanks his father "from the bottom of [his] heart for the generous support, extended over six years, which alone has enabled [him] to hang on." He also thanks him for waiting "not only without complaint but full of encouragement, while chance after chance slipped away and when the goal receded farthest from sight."[73] In reading this letter, one wonders if God was not using six years of closed doors to help heal Lewis's relationship with his father. In having to depend on his father for support and encouragement, Lewis humbly realized that his father did love and care for him. He also got a glimpse of God's love and support, although he may not have recognized it until years later.

Personal Ponderings

Closed Doors

Closed doors can be very confusing and discouraging. We wonder what God must be thinking. Surely, we must have been the best person for the job. Sometimes we never understand, but other times, like Reepicheep, we later find that we were being protected. Aslan is not ungrateful to Reepicheep, nor does he underestimate his abilities, rather he knows "they would do dreadful things" to mice "in that world." Aslan tells Reepicheep that in this case "others must lead."[74]

Many of us can relate to this experience. Several years ago, a job opening for an editing position at a Christian publishing company became available. The job was located in a state that had seemed to be calling to me for several months. The state's license plate repeatedly appeared as I drove on the roads; a Web site ad for that state appeared suddenly as a pop up; and whenever I turned on the news, that state always seemed to be mentioned. I interpreted all of these things as a calling for the job and believed that God wanted me to move and work at this company.

However, flying out to the company with my husband, being away from my children, and going through the interviews turned out to be a very trying and confusing experience. It was draining and tense, as interviews often are, but there was something else. It just did not feel right. I felt like an outsider, not in the sense of a newcomer, but that I did not belong.

Disappointment and Confusion

The morning after I returned, I got the call. "I am sorry, but it just doesn't seem like a good fit for us right now," the voice at the other line informed me.

"Really. Why not?" I probed in surprise.

"I am sorry. It just isn't a good fit."

That was it. After all that, all they could say was, "It isn't a good fit."

I was so confused. Why would God take me all the way out there and have us look at houses just for me to hear them say, "It isn't a good fit."

What was I suppose to tell my husband and kids who were expecting to move? They even told their teachers! How was I going to face them? What had I done wrong? God, I just don't understand! What do you want from me?

God Works in Strange Ways

It took me a long time to listen to the feelings I had experienced while I was visiting the company. God was speaking to me.

He was telling me that the environment was not good for me. I needed to trust those feelings. Like Reepicheep, I was being protected. It wasn't that I was incapable of doing the job, God just knew that it would not be good for me to work there.

Not long after the trip and the phone call, I read an article about the company. In the article, an employee was quoted as saying, "We have a lot of filters in place here to keep the wrong kind of people out." Perhaps I was the wrong kind of person.

But why the trip? Why did God take me there? The trip was not about the job but the opportunity to give a gift to my husband and me. God wanted to send us away alone to reconnect and feel his awesome presence. God gave us a vacation we never could have afforded on our own and a spiritual lesson as well. To quote Garth Brooks, "Some of God's greatest gifts are unanswered prayers."

Finding Purpose

When has a door been closed for you?

How did you feel?

When have you been asked to do something that you did not feel you could do?

What did you learn?

When has God protected you from something you greatly sought after?

Finding Scripture

Sometimes doors are closed to us because God has some place else for us. We may think we know best and may arrogantly convince ourselves that we are doing what God wants, but then God enters and redirects us—sometimes by spitting us out of the mouth of a whale. While God told Jonah to "go at once to Nineveh, that great city and cry out against it," Jonah convinced himself that he should go to Tarshish instead (Jon 1:1–3). However, God closed the doors of Tarshish to Jonah with a mighty storm.

As the storm tossed Jonah's ship around, the crew became frightened and wondered what caused it. On learning of Jonah's refusal to go to Nineveh they tossed him out into the raging waters, praying for his protection and hoping for the storm to end. God sent a large fish (like a whale) to swallow Jonah. Trapped in the belly of the fish, Jonah repented and promised to go Nineveh. "Then the LORD spoke to the fish, and it spewed Jonah out upon the dry land" (Jon 2:10).

Jonah kept his promise and converted Nineveh, but he then again thought that he knew better than God. When God grew convinced of their repentance and decided to change "his mind about the calamity that he had said he would bring upon them" (Jon 3:10), Jonah became angry with God. He wondered why he ever had to travel to Nineveh at all, if God did not intend to punish Nineveh. Like us, he questioned and grew frustrated with God's plans. He did not understand them.

Through Jonah's story, Lewis's experiences, and Reepicheep's closed doors, we come to understand our own closed doors. Our frustrations become a little more bearable, and we learn to wait patiently to see how God's plans will unfold. With time, we will likely realize that God knows best.

Suggested Scripture Reading and Reflections

Read the book of Jonah, and consider the times that you were frustrated and angry with God. Perhaps draw a picture of the whale that you currently feel trapped in.

When have you acted like Jonah by avoiding God and convincing yourself that you knew best?

How did God respond to you with closed doors? How did you feel?

When have you been confused, frustrated, and angered by God's plans?

How have these feelings trapped you in a whale?

What is your whale?

What do you need to do to convince God to have the whale spit you out?

Where do you think you will land?

What will you need to do once you are out?

Section Two
Holding on to Hope

[Love]…hopes all things.
1 Corinthians 13:7

Trusting What We Do See

Reflections on Lewis with Caspian

*T*rusting in what we see often gives us hope in times of turmoil. If we have the courage to believe in what we see when others do not, we might be able to lead others to hope. We might help them find comfort and direction when life seems dismal and hopeless.

Two sources provided Lewis with a different type of seeing throughout his life: Through nature and books, Lewis found hope in the most dismal of times. Although he did not recognize these windows as gifts from God until later in his life, he did believe in what he saw and shared his insights with others.

As mentioned previously, in *Surprised by Joy* we learn of the toy garden as Lewis's first experience of this. While many of us may have tossed the tin lid away in repulsion, Lewis found a strong connection to nature in the lid can piled with dirt, grass, and other outside wonders. It brought him joy and followed him through much of his life.

This sense of joy in nature also brought him comfort when he served in the infantry during World War I. In an October 1917 letter to Greeves, while stationed in Plymouth, Lewis writes of the beautiful scenery. In a time where most of the soldiers' eyes are focused on death and violence, Lewis directs his away "from the camp" to "a fine landscape—nice cozy little bits of green country with cottages and water and trees, then woodier hills rising at last into big, open moors that make up the horizon." He further remarks that the scenery "is especially lovely in the mists of early morning or of night."[1] In nature, he finds peace, solace, and hope in times of war.

Lewis also writes to his father on July 22, 1917, of his "effort to cling to the old life of books, hoping that [he] may save [his] soul alive," and again in January 1918, he uses his knowledge of books to find conversation "with a fellow of literary tastes" when he finds himself "back on a course of bombing."[2] When nature cannot provide hope, he turns inward to the beauty he has found in books and helps others find it as well. With those with whom he finds refuge in literary discourse, he also finds hope in envisioning continued conversation and friendship after the war. In a November 1917 letter to Greeves, he talks of his "good friend Johnson, whom [he] hope[s] to meet after the war as a scholar of Queens at Oxford."[3]

Lewis also used this type of seeing that he found in the tin lid when he faced the loss of his mother. Intuitively, he looked to nature and literature to cope with his grief. Although Lewis does not see God as helping him find hope until later in life, he does trust in what he sees through all of his life.

As an older and wiser man, it seems that he looks back at his life and reflects on this through the character of Lucy. Lewis realized that children often see what adults do not. In a letter to Ruth, one of his young fans who wrote to him just months before he died in 1963, he encourages her to find hope in her love for Jesus and affirms what she sees in Narnia. He tells her:

> If you continue to love Jesus, nothing much can go wrong with you, and I hope you may always do so. I'm so thankful you realized [the] "hidden story" in the Narnian books. It is odd, children nearly *always* do, grown-ups hardly ever.[4]

Lewis calls adults' attention to our lessened ability to see God as we grow up in the following Caspian scene. However, more importantly he gives children encouragement to trust in what they see—even when no one else sees or believes them.

Interestingly, in this letter to Ruth he also admits to embedding a "hidden story," that he wants us to find. In Narnia, Lewis wants us to see and trust in the Christian story of hope. And if we can't find it as adults, perhaps our children will help us notice it.

Personal Ponderings

Do You See What I See?

In *Prince Caspian,* Lucy shows us the frustration that children feel when adults do not see what they see. As she continues to believe that she saw Aslan, her eyes fill with tears even after the others vocally chastise and doubt her. Yet she firmly states, "But I know he was here." Not surprisingly the others continue to doubt her, and Peter responds, "Yes, Lu, but we don't, you see."

There is irony in Peter's words. As he continues to doubt, his concluding words are "you see." Lewis is having a little fun here, showing us that we can be our own worst enemies. We can be completely blind to something that is right in front of us— even when it comes through in our own words.

Lucy "cries bitterly" at the end of chapter 9 because she knows that she is right, and they will not believe her. But she does not stay in despair and lose sight of hope. Instead, she courageously trusts what she sees and finds her way to Aslan.

Lucy's experiences strongly speak of hope. They remind us of the times that we did trust in what we saw even when others did not see it and may have called us crazy. Remember the tears, the frustration, and the hurt, but also remember the great joy in knowing that you had correctly trusted in what you saw.

Couples often experience this as they fall in love. Family and friends do not always see what the couple sees. The doubts and questions came rolling in. "Why is he dating her? What does she see in him?" Like Lucy, many of us may experience tears of dismay and weariness in trying to make others understand why we would want a relationship with this person and contemplate marriage. We often trust our instinct and hope that all will work out well, and perhaps over the course of time others will realize they were wrong. God often leads us to see what others do not.

Marriage brings couples together to grow in faith and friendship. The commitment of serving each other and being there for one another through the best and worst of life's circumstances exemplifies a true sense of being soul mates. Love does not always make sense, nor does God. When following God's lead, you need to be able to see and believe in what you see. When doubt leads us astray, we must have the strength and the courage to hope for what we see to be true.

The Eyes of a Parent

Like married partners, parents also need to have the ability to see their children differently than others see them. This does not mean that we don't recognize our children's faults. Rather, it requires us to see qualities in our children more clearly and deeply than others—for it is our responsibility to make our children see and rise above their faults. With bifocals of hope, we are called to see the "greatness" and "lion-strength" that God has breathed into our children. With these bifocals, we find the ability to hope for what we know our children will become.

This becomes especially important as children learn and grow in environments that do not take the time to appreciate their "greatness" and "lion-strength." It wouldn't be fair to say others don't care, but like the other Pevensie children, they choose to see through eyes that are sometimes blind. As parents, we must have the courage and the hope to help others see differently.

As many of you know, parenting is one of the most difficult but rewarding tasks God puts before us. Finding Aslan with Lucy renews our hope and courage to believe in what we see. Lucy had the guidance and encouragement of Aslan; we have the help of God. We are not alone. We are called and challenged to make others see, but we are not alone.

We may reflect with Lucy ashamedly on our doubts and frustrations. As she tells Aslan, "I am sorry," we say the same to God. Together, we proudly proclaim with hope: "I am ready now."

Finding Purpose

When have you lost hope?
When have you seen something that others did not?
How did you deal with your frustrations?
What reward did you receive for holding out hope?
What are you most challenged with right now?
What must you make others see?
Why?

Finding Scripture

The book of Genesis shows us how God seemed to lose hope with his creation. In the story of Noah, God becomes angry at humanity's wickedness and decides to destroy all living creatures with a great flood, all except for Noah. God favored Noah and told him of his plan to destroy all of life on earth. God instructed him to build an ark and fill it with his wife, sons, his sons' wives, and two of every living creature (one female and one male). Those living around Noah must have thought him to be crazy as he built his large, multileveled ark and filled it with food and animals. However, Noah believed in what God told him. He had hope in God's promise to keep him safe. He trusted what he saw and heard. Because of this, Noah was saved.

After the flood ceased and the earth dried, God made a covenant with Noah never to wipe out all living beings with water. As a sign of this covenant, scripture tells us that God created the rainbow. Emerging after stormy and desolate weather, the rainbow continues to serve as a symbol of hope for us. It reminds us of God's covenant with Noah, but it also reminds us that, like Noah, if we trust in God we can weather any storm.

Suggested Scripture Reading and Reflections

Spend some time reading and reflecting on Genesis 6:5—9:17.

When have you believed in something that others would not?

How did you know that God was speaking to you?

Lewis often found hope in nature. Noah also found hope in the dove and the rainbow. When have you found hope in nature?

What struggles are you facing now?

How will you find hope?

Hurt by Hate

Reflections on Lewis with Caspian

*L*ewis directs our attention to hate through the character of Nikabrik. In chapter 5, Nikabrik shouts out about dwarfs, "I hate 'em. I hate 'em worse than the Humans." Unhealed from past hurts and living in fear, Nikabrik displaces his negative emotions onto dwarfs. He hates them and sees them as the embodiment of all his sufferings.[5]

In Nikabrik, we see Lewis working out his own experiences with hate. In *Surprised by Joy*, he recounts many school experiences with students called bloods that caused him to "hate Wyvern."[6] Lewis describes the bloods as using all means to humiliate and torment the boys beneath them. The system was "devised for protecting the strong against the weak."[7]

As one of the weak, Lewis found himself growing "more and more tired, both in body and mind."[8] In fact, he goes so far as to say that "never, except in the front-line trenches (and not always there)" did he experience such a "continuous weariness as at Wyvern."[9] Later in writing his autobiography, Lewis notes this experience as spiritually deadening, as "that school life was a life almost wholly dominated by the social struggle."[10] Lewis found a relief from the physical torment in his intelligence with literature, yet this he says turned him into an arrogant prig.[11]

In looking back at the experience and his fictional unpublished work *Loki Bound*, he sees himself in the character of Loki. He says, "Loki was a projection of myself; he voiced that sense of priggish superiority whereby I was, unfortunately, beginning to compensate myself for my unhappiness."[12] He also notes in the character of Loki the pessimism that led him to his atheism, which he calls "a whirl of contradictions." He was angry with God "for not existing" and also angry with God for "creating a world."[13] In his hatred of the bloods and Wyvern, Lewis began a path of spiritual darkness and death. Lewis describes this as "a coarse curtain which at any moment might be drawn aside to reveal all the heavens I then knew." Since he was able to pull open the curtain from time to time, he found moments of hope where "seconds of gold scattered in months of dross."[14] In these moments of hope, God worked and eventually brought Lewis back.

Do you not see glimpses of yourself and others in Lewis? Do we not also angrily lash out at God when life becomes wearisome? Don't we also hide behind our "coarse curtains" and miss out on the golden rays of hope? The danger is we may lurk behind the curtain too long and displace all of our pain, fear, and suffering onto one person or group of people. Essentially, the curtain blocks us from hope and from God. It keeps us from looking inward at ourselves and our own fears. Yet, that is exactly what we need to do in order to break the cycle of pain. Hating others causes others hurt, which results in them also lashing out in hate.

Unfortunately, Nikabrik, unlike Lewis, never reflects on his hate. His anger and fear lead him to black sorcery and a false hope in the White Witch. He loses all hope in Aslan. He lashes out in violence that results in the loss of his own life. I think in Nikabrik Lewis was looking at what would have been his own destiny had he never found his way back to God. He brings our attention to this when Caspian says, "I am sorry for Nikabrik though he hated me from the first moment he saw me. He had gone sour inside from long suffering and hating."[15]

In the tragedy of Nikabrik, one cannot help but see recent violent instances in our schools. In almost all of the shootings, someone was retaliating for past wrongs and hurts from which he had not healed. Charles Roberts took out his pain and hurt on innocent Amish girls. The note he left for his family revealed that he was haunted by the death of his premature daughter and sins of the past. He said that he was angry with God and thus lashed out in hate and violence. He lost all hope, took the lives of others, and ended his own life.

Other recent instances of violence also reveal unhealed pasts of perpetrators. For example, in the Virginia Tech shootings, Cho Seung-Hui openly fired on and killed fellow college students and professors. His suicide letter left behind mentioned a hatred of rich kids, debauchery, and deceitful charlatans.[16] Relatives revealed that Cho had a speech impediment for which he received ridicule from classmates.[17] Lewis also underwent humiliation and suffering in school. He also hated as a result. Fortunately, Lewis did not lash out violently, but ongoing school violence shows that many do.

Hate is real, and it needs to be understood and addressed. If we don't look inward at our fears, anger, and hate, we may find ourselves in the same situation as Nikabrik—"gone sour inside." Like Roberts and Cho, we may end up inflicting pain and suffering on others—continuing a cycle of pain, suffering, hate, and violence. We must begin to end the cycle by healing ourselves. Rather than lashing out in violent hate, we must reach out in a love that hopes to heal.

Personal Ponderings

Turn the Other Cheek

Sometimes we can witness and experience this hate in our own ethnically diverse neighborhoods. Although diversity could enrich us with many different cultures and traditions that could help us to break free from ignorance, sometimes this diversity brings a great deal of tension, turmoil, and hate. Often this stems from fear. Faced with diversity, we work to build territorial walls to keep others out. We fear that blending with others will cause us to lose our identity. We fear because we do not understand. In the midst of all this confusion, we blame each other and spread hate.

Recently, a family recounted their own neighborhood experience of this situation. A couple of children walked over to a neighborhood playground with their mother. While the mother sat on the bench and read, they played on the swings. After only a few minutes, the children returned unhappy and distressed.

"Those kids won't let us play here," Brianna wailed.

"She hit me," Emma complained holding her arm.

"Why? What happened?" inquired the mother while looking in the direction of the two children swinging.

"They said this is their playground, and we can't play here because we are white," Brianna angrily informed her mother.

"They are mean. I hate them," Emma declared.

At first the mother did not know what to say. Like her children, she was shocked and angered. The mother counted to ten and took a deep breath. She did not want her children to hate others.

"Emma, hate will not help with this. Jesus tells us to love everyone," she attempted to explain.

"But they are mean; I hate them," Emma repeated.

The mother thought to herself, "How can I help her understand the golden rule?" She followed by saying to her distraught daughter, "Did Jesus say to only love those who are nice to us?"

"No," Brianna looked down.

"What does Jesus tell us to do when people are mean to us?" the mother continued.

"Turn the other cheek," Brianna quietly replied still looking down and then glancing toward the swings.

"I am not turning my cheek when someone hits me. I am going to hit them back," Emma huffily replied in exasperation and then continued, "I need to protect myself."

Clearly, she was not getting the point.

"Emma, those girls have probably had someone tell them that they can't play somewhere because of their color. They are angry and taking it out on you," the mother tried explaining.

Emma just looked at her in silence for a few minutes and responded, "But that is not fair. I didn't do anything to them."

"I know," the mother replied. "But that is how hurt and hate work. The only way to stop it is by doing what Jesus taught us. We have to love and hope that they will learn to love and stop hating."

Emma and Brianna nodded, and then said, "Let's go home."

This is a constant lesson for us. We do not stop hating overnight. With every fear and flare up of anger, we are tempted to hate. We still fight with each other, but by taking these little opportunities to reflect on our hurts and fears and try to understand them, we begin to turn the cycle around. Like Jesus tells us in the Bible, we need to rise above the situation and treat others as we want to be treated. We must turn the other cheek. Sometimes this means walking away in silence.

Finding Purpose

When have you felt hate directed toward you?
How did you respond?
When have you lashed out in hate?
What was the result?
What hurts from the past lead you to fear, anger, and hate?
What "coarse curtain" are you hiding behind?
What glimmers of hope could you focus on?
How can you begin to heal?
Where can you find love?

Finding Scripture

The tragedy of Cain and Abel warns us of the dangers of resentment and hatred. When God finds favor with Abel's offering and not Cain's, Cain reacts with hostility. God asks Cain why he is angry and advises him "to do well" and that if he does not do well and get over his anger and hateful feelings "sin is lurking at the door." God tells Cain that sin desires him and that he must "master" it (Gen 4:7). However, Cain does not listen to God. Instead, he gives into his resentment and takes Abel into the field and kills him. Sin becomes Cain's master. He loses the ability to grow crops in the soil and becomes a lonely wanderer without the presence of God.

Through Cain, we see our own sinful vengeances that distance us from God and others. In God's words to Cain, we see hope. While sin seeks to master us, we can master it. We must learn from Cain's mistakes and rise above our hateful and angry emotions. If we let our hate rule us, we will find the same fate as Cain: a lonely wanderer without God.

Lewis found himself on this path for many years. Although he did not kill anyone, his anger and hate led him on a lonely path away from God. Don't we also find ourselves heading in this direction?

Suggested Scripture Reading and Reflections

As you read Genesis 4:1–16, reflect on the times that you have acted like Cain.

When have you felt like Cain?

How can we become the master of sin, as God advises?

When has your hate made you a lonely wanderer, distanced from God?

How can you find yourself back to God?

How have you in the past?

Mistakes of the Past

Reflections on Lewis with Caspian

*A*dmitting that we have made a mistake is not easy. In fact, our first inclination is to point the finger elsewhere and find faults in others. Yet, we are called to forgive. Lewis speaks of this in a letter to his friend Malcolm as he reflects on the challenge of "forgive us our trespasses as we forgive those who trespass against us" in the Lord's Prayer. He admits that "to go on forgiving, to forgive the same offence every time" is "the real tussle." And I think most of us would agree with him. It is hard to keep forgiving, especially the same offence. However, Lewis shares some advice: "If I find it difficult to forgive those who bullied me at school, let me, at that very moment, remember, and pray for, those I bullied."[18] In reflecting on how we have hurt others and our own need for forgiveness, we humbly find ourselves willing to forgive others. We learn to look inward and hold ourselves accountable for our own actions.

Admitting Our Faults

Lewis exemplifies this lesson when Lucy finds Aslan. After rejoicing and sobbing with delight, Lucy begins to blame the others for her not finding Aslan sooner. She says to Aslan, "Wasn't it a shame? I saw you all right. They wouldn't believe me. They're all so—"

Aslan interrupts her with "the faintest suggestion of a growl" that shows his disapproval. Lucy gets the point and quickly says, "I'm sorry." Like us, though, she follows her apology with the infamous "but" clause that still attempts to shift blame. "I didn't

73

mean to start slanging the others. **But it wasn't my fault anyway, was it?**"[19] Don't you hear yourself here? How often have you also said it wasn't your fault?

Like Jesus, Aslan will not accept this. He "looked straight into her eyes"—just as God looks straight into our souls. Lucy continues; this time she gives her excuses. "You don't mean it was? How could I—I couldn't have left the others and come up to you alone, how could I?"[20] Don't we do this also? After the "but" clause, we list all our excuses in an attempt to justify our actions or nonactions. Lewis helps us see ourselves so clearly here. He shows our stages of denial for accepting blame.

1. It wasn't me!
2. But…
3. How could I have…

Like Aslan, God does not fall for any of this. He expects us to take full ownership for our mistakes. Lucy finally finds this in Aslan's look. "Don't look at me like that…oh well, I suppose I *could*. Yes, and it wouldn't have been alone, I know, not if I was with you. But what would have been the good?"[21]

Here Lucy begins to take responsibility and realize that none of the excuses hold true. Aslan would have been there to help her. Here is our lesson. Not only must we take responsibility and ownership for our mistakes, we also must realize that everything is possible with God. We are never alone. God is always there beside us. Therefore, no excuse will ever hold muster with God.

Lucy finally presents this lesson to us clearly: "You mean that it would have turned out all right—somehow?"[22] But like us, as soon as she learns the lesson, she wants to look back again and change things. Instead of looking forward and learning, she dwells on her mistakes. This is where most of us get stuck: living and dwelling in our mistakes of the past.

Lucy wants to know what would have happened had she followed. Aslan pushes her out of the past and forward. He helps her move beyond despair and gives her hope.

> To know what *would* have happened, child? No. Nobody is ever told that. But anyone can find out what will happen. If you go back to the others now, and wake them up; and tell them you have seen me again; and that you must all get up at once and follow me—what will happen? There is only one way of finding out.[23]

We can also learn from this. Like Lucy we need to forget about what *would* have been and focus on what *will* be if we learn from the past and try again. God gives us the glorious gift of forgiveness. We have a second chance to get it right. That is where we must put our energy. But as we saw in this scene with Lucy, this is not an easy task. It takes the help of God and the wisdom of the Holy Spirit.

If you remember, after Lucy finds Aslan before their conversation, Aslan licks her nose and breathes on her. She felt "his warm breath [come] all around her" and then she "gazed up into the large wise face."[24] Once again, Lewis calls us to remember our anointing with the Holy Spirit. With this scene, he helps us to remember the gifts we received when we were marked with the wet, oily mark of the Holy Spirit and felt his warm, fiery breath. Like Lucy, this gave us the ability to hear, see, and feel God so that we also could find the wisdom we need to grow and learn. The Holy Spirit gives us the strength to push out of the despair of the past and into the future with hope.

Personal Ponderings

Leaving the Past Behind

As a parent, I am constantly called to teach this lesson to my children. On an hourly basis, I hear refrains of: "Not me; wasn't me; I didn't do it." Then, if a suspect finally emerges, I get the "but" and the litany of excuses. It is exhausting yet necessary to help them admit their mistakes and move on. Once they do admit, like Aslan and Christ, I must help them see beyond their despair and disappointment and look to the lesson for the future. Perhaps the best way to teach this is to lead by example.

Leading by Example

I have found that sharing my own mistakes often speaks more clearly and kindly to my children. They learn to see me as human and imperfect, like themselves. One of my deepest regrets taught me to listen to my inner voice and trust my instincts.

After Easter Sunday Mass a number of years ago, we went over to my parents' home. As my siblings arrived, my sister Natalie said, "We should go see Ralph!" (Ralph was our great uncle but we all saw him as a grandfather.) I had also been feeling that we should see Ralph and agreed. But (the infamous "but clause") we got lost in the busyness of the day and none of us went to visit Ralph. A few days later, Ralph died. All of us regretted not visiting him. We lost our chance to say goodbye. Like Lucy, we began with the excuses: "We were busy. Ralph wasn't feeling well. We didn't know…"

Then once we realized there was no good excuse to hide our mistake, we dwelled on the what would have happened. Of course, we couldn't go back and focusing on the *would* kept us from pushing forward. Instead, we had to focus on the *will*.

We all learned about the need to make the time to visit loved ones because we are never guaranteed that there will be a tomorrow. I have learned to listen to my inner voice and instincts more.

The *will* pushed me to help others see Ralph the way I saw him. I could not go back to visit Ralph personally, but I could write him a loving tribute that let others remember him at his funeral. I pushed forward with hope and wrote a eulogy that I gave at his funeral. Perhaps recalling this type of experience will push you to remember the loved ones who have made a difference in your life.

Finding Purpose

When have you attempted to shift blame on to others?

What mistakes do you need to leave in the past?

How will you move beyond the *would* and find hope to
focus on the *will*?

Finding Scripture

Casting Stones

Jesus makes it very clear on several occasions that we are not to judge or cast stones. We are to look inward at our own misdeeds. The lesson that comes most often to mind is when the church leaders are about to stone a woman for adultery, and Jesus instructs those who are without any sin to cast the first stone. Not surprisingly, they all drop their stones and leave. That is because we are all guilty of sin.

Loving Others

Like John, Luke also gives us Jesus's directions on how we are to act when others hurt us or engage in sinful actions. Not surprisingly, we hear that we need to love our enemies and focus on our own actions and sins. God alone is fit to judge the actions of others. The themes of forgiveness, reconciliation, and non-judgmental attitudes toward others are constant and a constitutive part of this gospel message. These are suggestions not to be taken lightly; they form the core identity of discipleship.

Suggested Scripture Reading and Reflections

Read John 8:1–8 and reflect on the actions of the Pharisees and Jesus's treatment of the sinful woman.

When have you been quick to cast stones?

How many stones would you have thrown if you had reflected on your own mistakes?

When are you most likely to cast stones? Why?

What steps can you take to be more understanding of others?

Read Luke 6:27–42 and focus on the command of loving one's enemies.

Why does Jesus want us to love our enemies?

When have you found it most challenging to love an enemy?

What did you do?

When have you judged someone else's actions?

What was the result?

How might the situation have been different if you had looked inward?

What would have happened if you prayed for someone you
had hurt in a similar way?

Why is it hard to look at our own mistakes and take
accountability?

Courageous Change

Reflections on Lewis with Caspian

Change does not come easy. Many of us fear change. We like
to cling to what is comfortable and familiar. When something
works, we want it to keep working the same way. However, life
does not work that way and neither does sharing our faith with
others. Christ calls us to reach beyond our paradigms and find new
ways to minister to others. He calls us to embrace change. That is
why Jesus met such hostility with the Pharisees, Sadducees, and
other religious leaders of his time. He called into question many of
their customs, laws, and traditions. He wanted them to change.

In reading Lewis's letters to Malcolm, we may be touched to
hear Lewis voice his own struggles with change. Articulately, he
philosophically traces our problem with change back to our erro-
neous judgment that a past, good experience was the perfect
experience. We set that experience "up as the norm" for comparing all future events. The problem with this is that by living in the
past and refusing to open ourselves up to change, we may "reject
the good that God offers us" because we are too busy "expecting
some other good" that we believe must be the same as the past.[25]

Wisely, Lewis remarks that always looking back at the past
only causes us torment. In refusing to see the new blessings of the
present that God brings with change, we turn our "golden moments

in the past" into a "tormenting...norm." Lewis advises that instead: "Leave the bulbs alone, and the new flowers will come up." Memories securely imbedded in the past will allow new flowers to bloom. We just need to be open to new blossoms. We need to see how change can bring a new beauty of its own.[26]

Never the Same Way Twice

Lewis helps us work through our fears of change with Lucy. When she realizes that the others will not see Aslan as they did the last time they were in Narnia, she begins to fear. She says:

> Oh dear, oh dear. And I was so pleased at finding you again. And I thought you'd let me stay. And I thought you'd come roaring in and frighten all the enemies away—like last time. And now everything is going to be horrid.[27]

Lucy is afraid. She had planned for Aslan to come in and act in the same way he did last time they found conflict in Narnia. She had not planned on change. She had not planned on having to convince others, especially when they would not be able to see Aslan. How would she convince them?

However, like God, Aslan has a way of soothing her fears and helping her to find strength and hope. He understands Lucy's weaknesses and helps her to understand: "It is hard for you, little one. But things never happen the same way twice." Lucy then buries her head in Aslan's mane and "she could feel lion-strength going into her." That lion-strength fills her with hope and courage. She "suddenly sat up" and said, "I'm sorry, Aslan. I'm ready now." Aslan in turn looks at her and acknowledges her change. "Now you are a lioness. And now all Narnia will be renewed. But come. We have no time to lose."[28]

Personal Ponderings

Lion-Strength

Some of the scariest changes that we are called to make involve money, especially when we know the change will bring less money. This happens frequently in families when one of the spouses decides to stay at home to raise children and work from home doing contract or freelance work. A steady paycheck is traded for spending more time with children while they grow and develop.

Although parents know that their decision is right, worries still rear their ugly heads in the turmoil of every day life. Often these worries give way to tears and despair in the midst of tormenting questions: How will we pay the bills? Will I ever be able to return to work? What do my friends and family really think? How can I balance all of this and stay sane? Like Lucy, in the midst of doubt and challenge, we may feel afraid.

But while God has a way of creating catalysts to make us change, he also offers us the lion-strength to deal with the obstacles, doubts, questions, and fears. There will likely be moments of tension and frustration. Sometimes, we will lash out in anger at friends and family members. However, lion-strength enables us to say, "I am sorry" (like Lucy) and continue forward with what God is calling us to do.

Gifts of Strength

Many of us can recall stories and moments in our lives when God made it evident that change was necessary. You also were transformed with lion-strength. God has given us many gifts that provide us with this strength.

The sacraments offer moments and occasions to be renewed like Lucy. The weekly celebration of the Holy Eucharist draws us closer to God and unites us together in worship as a parish community in order that together we become one in the body of Christ. We share each other's struggles and challenges and find strength in unity.

The sacrament of reconciliation is a way to find the courage to go to God and say, "I am sorry," like Lucy said to Aslan. Have you not also felt renewed with a new strength and energy in this experience? Did you not find yourself able to say, "I am ready now," when previously you were paralyzed with fear and despair. Finding the lion-strength for the courage to change is a powerful and freeing experience.

Like Aslan, God continues to challenge us and is always there for us. God never expects us to go out alone into the unknown. Like Lucy, all we have to do is reach out and bury ourselves in God's mane so that we can also become lions and lionesses.

Finding Purpose

When have you felt yourself faced with a need for change? How did you react?

How did God give you the lion-strength you needed?

When have you buried yourself in God's mane and become a lioness or lion?

What change is God calling you to make now?

Where will you find the strength and courage to make that change?

Finding Scripture

Jesus found much conflict with the scribes, Pharisees, and religious leaders of his time because he called for changes in their hearts. In fulfilling the prophecy of the Old Testament, he brought understanding and changes that called many of the old ways into question. In Matthew, we find that Jesus's teaching calls us to "a complete change of heart and conduct."[29] Very often, Jesus did this by expanding on and clarifying the laws that were laid down by Moses in the Old Testament.

One such example occurs during the Sermon on the Mount. The Pharisees were not happy with Jesus's adaptations and calls for change. Thus, they clung to the security of the past and attempted to silence Jesus's call for change by killing him. Their preoccupation with the past blinded them to the presence of God who stood in their midst. God's words fell on deaf ears. How often do we do the same in our refusal to see the blessing of change?

Suggested Scripture Reading and Reflections

Read Jesus's Sermon on the Mount in Matthew 5—7.

How does Jesus elaborate on the laws of Moses?
What changes does he call for?
Why would the Pharisees fear these changes?
Based on the teachings of Jesus, what changes do you need to make?
Which changes will be the most difficult for you? Why?
What necessary steps will it take to change?

Like a Little Child

Reflections on Lewis with Caspian

*I*n reading the Narnia stories, it becomes readily apparent that Lewis understood and adored children. In Narnia, he personifies Jesus's words that we must be like little children to enter the kingdom of heaven for they are the only ones who find it and enter.

We also see Lewis's admiration and respect of children in the letters that he wrote them. All of the letters show Lewis's ability to speak to them as fellow scholars. He never speaks down to or patronizes them. He addresses their questions with the same depth and intellectualism that he does with all of his adult correspondence. He admires and appreciates their wisdom. Their gifts and pictures he appreciatively accepts with admiration. He points out their ability to understand the spiritual "supposals" of the Narnia series—as many of the adults don't always understand the Christian message. And most importantly, he frequently asks his children readers to pray for him. Lewis does all of these things because he takes Jesus's words to heart. In Narnia, he hopes that we will also find this lesson.

Acting without Question

In chapter 11, Lewis gives us a glimpse of how we are to act if we are to be like little children. Shortly after the Pevensie children reunite with Aslan and seconds after Trumpkin decides he can trust Aslan, the children and the dwarf are all called into action. Aslan calls their attention to the moon setting and dawn beginning. He then says to Peter, Trumpkin, and Edmund, "We have no time to lose," and asks them to "hasten into the mound and deal with what [they] will find there." Immediately upon hearing Aslan's words they "drew their swords and saluted, then turned and jingled away into the dusk."[30]

When was the last time that God asked you to do something and you immediately acted without question or contemplation? Only a child would have the courage to go and follow those orders without asking the how, what, and why. Only a child would not fear what was to be found there. As Lewis reminds us here, children seem to have a natural hope and trust in their abilities. They do not fear that they will not be able to do something. They just do it to our fear and amazement as we watch them climb to the top of the jungle gym and then hang from their knees laughing in joy and freedom.

Personal Ponderings

Socks for Jesus

Children are often fascinated with nativity scenes. Inspired by the example of St. Francis of Assisi with the first crèche display as a way to teach about the incarnation of Jesus as the word becoming flesh and dwelling among us, the depiction of a newborn baby is apt for Christmas—a season of hope and childlike faith. The following story shows us how this image of the newborn Christ can call us to help others in need.

In the midst of Advent, a young child looked with admiration and love at the baby Jesus at the parish nativity display. Noticing that baby Jesus's feet were not covered by his blanket, she worried that he might be cold. It was winter, after all. Seeing artificial snow nearby, she gently covered his feet and body with the cotton snow thinking now he will be warm.

Later, during Mass, the parish asked parishioners to bring a Christmas gift for the poor of the community. The mother explained to her child that this is "giving a gift to Jesus." Thinking about what Jesus needed most, the young child excitedly decided on the perfect gift: a pair of socks to keep Jesus's feet warm. The mother helped the little girl wrap up a pair of wool socks and watched as her daughter carried the wrapped package up to the altar. As the little girl placed the gift beside Jesus in the manger, she whispered, "Now your feet will be warm, Jesus."

Acts of Hope

While Jesus's feet did not need socks, someone else may have. God can work through us, especially in the experience of young and innocent children to teach us important truths about the meaning of life. This story illustrates how a family learned to keep someone else's feet warm. Sometimes a seemingly simple gift can be a profound learning and teachable moment for adults to see through the eyes of child.

While we often give in to worries and anxiety about money and gifts during the Christmas season, focusing on what we will give to Jesus causes us to reexamine the true meaning of the season. Thinking in this way may help us to find hope and love in the act of giving. Could Lewis have known that the word *jingle* would pull us back to reexamine the true meaning of Christmas—a season of hope and love?

Finding Purpose

As a child, when did you act with hope and love?
How can you hold on to the ability to hope like a child?
What is God calling you to do today?
How will you act with hope?

Finding Scripture

Called to Battle

The Old Testament comes to mind with Lewis's depiction of Peter, Edmund, and Trumpkin's loyalty and bravery. In 1 Samuel 17, we see another youth who courageously acts without question. David valiantly takes on Goliath without ever fearing or wondering how he will defeat a skilled warrior who stands six-and-a-half-feet tall. Angered by Goliath's insults of God's army, David tells Saul that he will defend Israel in battle against Goliath.

Saul questions how a youth such as David with no battle experience could possibly survive against a warrior like Goliath. David finds hope in his past victories over a lion and a bear and believes that the Lord who protected him in those battles will also keep him safe in battle with Goliath. David does not wonder how, nor does he fear. He hears God's call and acts out of faith. In return, God does protect David and helps him defeat Goliath with a simple stone and sling. Through David's courage and faith, God brought hope to Israel.

Suggested Scripture Reading and Reflections

Read 1 Samuel 17 and reflect on the personal character of David.

What makes him so confident and hopeful?
How can you also act with faith, hope, and courage when
   God calls you?
What challenges have you overcome in the past?
How has God helped you in those challenges?
With what strengths has God blessed you?
How have you used them to do God's will?

How do you usually respond when God calls you to act?
David found hope and courage in reflecting on God's protection during past encounters with danger; what could you reflect on to find this hope and courage?
The other soldiers were afraid to battle Goliath. Do you think this had to do with their age?
Why do we lose confidence and hope as we grow older?
How can we hold on to the hope and courage of our youth?

Running Away

Reflections on Lewis with Caspian

*R*eading both *Mere Christianity* and *Prince Caspian* enables us to see that Lewis uses Narnia to personify the Christian struggles that he discusses in his reflections on Christianity. In his reflections on hope and faith, Lewis reasons that we lose hope in this world when we focus and look only at this world, which could never satisfy the longings that our souls desire. He suggests that this world was never intended to satisfy us, but rather to give us a glimpse of what is to come. If we are to find happiness, we must make it our goal to move on to the next life—the eternal life for which we were made—and to help others to find that life. If we see this life and world as the end, we are destined for unhappiness for it was never intended to satisfy us fully. Putting our hope in this world sets us up for failure and hopelessness.[31]

Although most of us can accept this explanation, we run into problems when we face adversity and hardship. That is when our faith begins to waver. To remain strong, we must surround ourselves with others who believe. Our faith needs to be nourished with prayer, scripture, and regularly attending Mass. Without these things, Lewis explains that our faith will starve, and we may wander off.

Yet, there is more. Lewis points out that even in feeding our faith, we are likely to find moments of failure. No matter how hard we try, we will fail. This is because we cannot do it alone. We can only do it with God. This realization brings us to the humble conclusion that we must let go of ourselves—our independence. We must let go of our way and trust in God's way. And in letting go, we must not stop trying, but rather we must try to do all that he says. We must listen to him and accept his advice.[32]

Fight or Flight

Lewis personifies these struggles with hope and faith in Prince Caspian when Doctor Cornelius tells Caspian and the others that Miraz is on the move. Upon his arrival, Doctor Cornelius explains that Miraz has realized that Old Narnia is not dead, and they are in imminent danger. In hearing the bad news, Nikabrik immediately becomes anxious and only sees two options—fight or flight. Can you not see yourself here? How often do we fill with adrenaline when sensing danger and conflict? How often do we fill with fear and anxiety? Here, I believe Lewis meant us to find ourselves. He intended to show us our tendency to lose sight of the larger picture.

However, Doctor Cornelius, believing in the Old Narnia and remembering the power and promises of Aslan, eases the group's fears. He redirects Nikabrik's idea of running by suggesting they move "east and down the river" toward Aslan's How. By recalling the location of where Aslan defeated the White Witch and came back to life and seeking refuge there, Doctor Cornelius instills hope. He feeds their faith in Aslan, and they find renewed hope. Even Nikabrik is quieted for the time being.[33]

In this conflict, Lewis shows us that we can offer hope to each other. In times of trouble, we need to seek out the refuge of God, as they sought refuge at Aslan's How. Jesus died and rose like Aslan. In the miracle of his resurrection, we were saved and given eternal life. Only there can we find hope and protection from death. In Narnia, Lewis shows us not only our struggles, but he also attempts to help us find our way home.

Personal Ponderings

Overwhelmed with Despair

I remember the first time I decided to run away. My mother had ordered me to clean my room. I remember looking through the doorway of my bedroom and seeing an empty Mr. Chuckles—a giant, plastic, yellow, smiley face whose mouth opened into a toy box. My toys completely covered my blue carpet. A sense of dread overwhelmed me. The task of cleaning up all of those toys seemed insurmountable. I climbed on to the top of Mr. Chuckles and sat there.

"No! I don't want to clean my room," I folded my arms and yelled with a pout.

"Get down from there. I want those toys picked up and put away," Mom responded.

"No. It will take too long," I reasoned.

"You are not coming out of your room until you finish," Mom replied and closed my door.

The sound of the door closing sealed my fate. I looked around at the toys and began to cry. The task seemed too hard to complete. I would never finish. I would be locked in my messy room of toys forever. I decided to escape from my prison. I was running away.

I pulled out my little floral suitcase from my closet, shoved in lots of clothes and books, and waved to Mr. Chuckles as I left. I remember walking out the front door with tears running down my face. I pulled my suitcase all the way to the top of hill—then I realized I had nowhere to go.

I set the suitcase down on the curb and sat on top of it. I looked down the hill at my house and thought, "She will be sorry. It is all her fault. I am never going home." More tears fell as I sat there waiting for my mom to come and beg me to come home. But she never came. I sat and sat and sat. Soon the tears stopped, and I took out a book and began to read. The neighbors must have had fun watching from the windows.

After finishing my books, I began to realize no one was coming. Mom was not going to beg me to return. My stomach began to rumble. I had no idea how long I sat up there, but it had seemed like an eternity. And it would soon be supper. What would I eat? Where would I sleep? I wanted to go home, but what about that messy room?

My stomach must have won out in the end because I headed home. To my surprise, mom was at the door. She took my suitcase and walked me to my room. "Come on. Let's clean your room," she said. She didn't yell at me for leaving my room or running away. She did not even mention it, nor did I. Together, we picked up my toys and fed Mr. Chuckles. I learned that independence and freedom were not the answer. Sometimes we just need a little help.

Doctor Cornelius was wise in getting Caspian and the others to rethink Nikabrik's plan of running. Wisely and symbolically, Lewis has Doctor Cornelius lead them to Aslan's How. Instead of running aimlessly, they plan to seek help from Aslan who has saved and protected Narnia in the past. Recalling Aslan's How as the Stone Table where Aslan rose from death, do we not also see this as God's How? When we feel like running do we not also find ourselves seeking the stone table where we will find help?

God's How

Unfortunately, our lessons often must be relearned. As adults, we still find ourselves giving in to a sense of hopelessness in difficult times. No matter how many lessons God gives us, we still have moments where we feel overwhelmed. This is part of being human. We lose hope so easily and become discouraged. Lewis found that it is during those times that we realize that we can't do it on our own—we must rely on God. We need his help.[34]

Like Caspian, many of us find support and strength from family and friends. Through them, we often receive wise counsel. Like the Narnia characters sought refuge at Aslan's How, we find refuge in God's How. He always comes through at the right moment to show us how to overcome adversity. God always leads us home and provides us with the help needed to meet the challenges that we face. We cannot do it alone. As Lewis eloquently explained in *Mere Christianity* and displays through his characters in Narnia, we need God to lead us home.

Oftentimes these challenges provide us with wisdom and experience to help others. Sometimes we need to run in order to learn to stay. Within the word *hopeless* is the word *hope*. Ironically, sometimes God lets us feel hopeless so that we can find hope.

Finding Purpose

When have you felt hopeless and wanted to run away?
How did God lead you back home?
Where did you find God's How?
When have you shared your experiences of hopelessness to
  help others find hope?

Finding Scripture

Jesus knew that we would deal with these struggles of independence. He knew that we would place our faith and hope in treasures of this world. To help us rethink our worldly ways, he offers us a parable of hope. In Luke, we hear the parable of the prodigal son. In that story, we meet ourselves in the son who demanded all of his inheritance from his father and then left to live on his own. Like many of us, the son assumed that money and freedom would bring him happiness. He also thought that he could survive on his own without his father. However, without guidance, his fortune quickly runs out. He squanders it on happiness that does not last. As a result, he finds himself alone, hungry, homeless, and unhappy.

Out of desperation, he works for a farmer taking care of pigs. Seeing that the pigs are happier than he is, he humbly returns to his father—a man who treats his workers very well—and begs him for work as a hired hand. His father rejoices at his return and throws him a celebration. All is forgiven.

How often have we been like the son? Do we not also arrogantly think that we can find happiness on our own away from God? Do we not rely on our own independence and material possessions for happiness and survival? When things get tough, what do we do? Do we not also also turn to God and others for help?

Here Jesus shows us that God realizes this about us. While the prodigal son is shown as foolish in his actions, we are also repeatedly foolish. Yet, God, our Father, will rejoice at our return. He wants to help us. With him and only with him, we will find true security and happiness. While he gives us the free will to rely on ourselves and allows us to seek material possessions for happiness, he will take us back time and again when we realize we were wrong. He wants us to rely fully on him for he knows that only with him will we find the happiness our soul desires. With God, there is hope.

St. Paul also reminds us that we are the body of Christ, and when one member suffers, the whole body suffers. We are all part of one body; we can also find this help and happiness by worshiping together in a community. This is why it is not enough to pray to God alone. We need to be part of a family. When we wander out alone, we become disconnected. As members of a family, we offer hope and guidance to one another. This is how God works in us and through us. We just need to let him. Like the prodigal son and the characters in Narnia, we need to humbly accept that we cannot go it all alone. We need help.

Suggested Scripture Reading and Reflections

Read Luke 15:11–24 and reflect on the times that you have wandered out alone.

When have you wandered off alone like the son?

What was the result?

Why is it so hard to depend on God rather than this world?

When have you relied on God and others for help?

What does this parable teach us about God?

What does Jesus reveal to us in this parable?

What portrait does he paint for us about God?

Fighting Fear

Reflections on Lewis with Caspian

*W*hen most of us think of our fears, we know we must get over them because they hold us back from fully partaking in life, but we don't necessarily connect them with morality. In *Mere Christianity*, Lewis logically discusses how our fears are intricately connected to our moral living and thus of great importance. Wisely, he reasons that no matter what sort of changes we work for socially, they may be in vain "unless we realize that nothing but the *courage* and *unselfishness* of individuals is ever going to make any system work properly."[35] To make these types of changes, Lewis tells us we must look "inside the individual." And in looking inward, we will find that fear most often leads to our immoral acts causing us to lash out selfishly and without courage.

Lewis's discussion of morality logically leads to an explanation of the cardinal virtues. In considering fear, fortitude represents two "kinds of courage—the kind that faces danger as well as the kind that 'sticks it' under pain." Whereas all of the virtues are important in Christian living, fortitude becomes particularly paramount because "you cannot practice any of the other virtues very long without bringing this one into play."[36] Lewis does exactly that by bringing fortitude into play in the story of Prince Caspian. He does this to remind us of our own fears, to let us see how and why fear must be conquered. By seeing other characters in action, we see ourselves. Through literature, Lewis used the talents God gave him to further Christianity. Believing that "the real job of the moral teacher is to keep on bringing us back, time after time, to the old simple principles which we are all anxious not to see,"[37] Lewis forces us to go back and look at ourselves through the characters of Narnia.

In doing so, Lewis displays characters struggling with the two types of courage we must work to maintain: (1) the ability to face danger; (2) the ability to follow courageously what we know to be true and just.

It Is All Lies

We see our fear to face danger in the character of Caspian when Doctor Cornelius tells Caspian where to find Cair Paravel. Caspian shudders and says, "Do you mean in the Black Woods? Where all the—the—you know, the ghosts live?" In Caspian's fears of ghosts in the woods, Lewis addresses one of the largest obstacles and challenges of our faith—an obstacle of hope. Is that not what fear really is? Will an absence of hope and faith allow God to protect us? Doesn't this show an emphasis on the earthly world and a lack of faith and hope in the eternal world Jesus promised us? As Doctor Cornelius responds to Caspian, he explains, "But it is all lies. There are no ghosts there. That is a story invented by the Telmarines."[38]

Essentially, Lewis reminds us here of what Christ tells us repeatedly in scripture. Fear is the tool of the devil. The Telmarines invented a story to keep people away from Cair Paravel. Satan works in the same way. He feeds us lies to keep us from doing good. He uses fear to chip away at our faith and hopes to cut us off from God. All of these lies feed on fear. Thus, to overcome our fear, we must rely on what we know to be true. We must use the voice of the Holy Spirit, prayer, scripture, and the advice of other Christians to sort out the truth from the lies.

Lewis shows us this through Doctor Cornelius's counseling of Caspian with the stories of the past and his handing Caspian "the greatest and most sacred treasure of Narnia"—Susan's horn. Doctor Cornelius tells Caspian that whoever blows the horn will receive "strange help."[39] Here, Lewis symbolically parallels the counsel of other Christians in Doctor Cornelius, scripture with the stories of Narnia, and the horn shows our ability to seek help from God in prayer. He goes on to show us the power of the Holy Spirit in the scene where the Pevensie children reunite with Aslan.

The Breath of Courage

This can be very difficult though because our selfishness and fear often leads us to want us to believe the lies. We try to convince ourselves that lies are the truth because they are easier to believe. We rationalize that the easier and more attractive path is the correct path. We become confused about how to act because we want to believe that the more convenient path is the correct path.

In this case, fear keeps us from listening to and trusting our true instincts. It holds us back from doing God's work. Lewis shows us this with Susan when Lucy urges her siblings to follow her to Aslan. Susan fights Lucy every step of the way. She lets fear rule her better judgment and spirals down the path of suffering. We see her fear lead to anger as she lashes out at Lucy. She begins by trying to discredit her in front of Peter and Edmund by accusing her of talking "nonsense" and "being downright naughty."[40] Haven't we done the same? Haven't we tried to make our own fears look like someone else's inadequacies? Guiltily, I must admit that I have used this defense mechanism.

When that does not work, Susan becomes more angry and hurtful toward Lucy. In fact, Lewis says "Susan was the worst." Have you ever been the worst? I wish I haven't, but I know I have. Then we witness Susan make fun of Lucy by saying, "Supposing I started behaving like Lucy; I might threaten to stay here whether the rest of you went on or not. I jolly well think I shall." Hurt by Susan's words and actions, Lucy "went first, biting her lip and trying not to say all things she thought of saying to Susan."[41] Lucy, still carrying Aslan's warm fiery breath, kept her eyes on Aslan.

Susan and Lucy could have broken out into a rather nasty fight here, the kind of fight with which Satan loves to distract us, especially when we are called to follow God in courage. Have you ever noticed that you are tried the most when you are called to do God's will? That is no coincidence. Satan uses his greatest tool, fear, to distract us and keep us from finding God. If Lucy had not ignored Susan's hurtful ranting of fear, the children might never have found Aslan. However, Lucy prevailed and led the group to Aslan.

After a short reunion of joy, Aslan calls Susan "in a deep voice," and helps her recognize and acknowledge her fear. In tears, Susan listens as Aslan says, "You have listened to fears, child. Come let me breathe on you. Forget them." Like Lucy, Aslan breathes on Susan with a breath of fiery courage. Susan is told to "forget" her fears.[42]

Jesus left us with this same breath of fiery courage—the Holy Spirit. He has also breathed on us. You have felt it? Haven't you? Haven't you found courage and strength at a time when you needed it most—a courage you normally don't have? To do God's will and follow him, we must ignore the voices of fear. Like Susan, we must "forget them," and like Lucy we must "bite our lips," at the fearful and angry accusations hurled around us. We must avoid lashing out in revenge and anger; instead, we must find the courage we have been given, keep our eyes on God, and lead others to him.

Personal Ponderings

Suffering from Fear

Listening to Caspian and Doctor Cornelius, we are reminded of how childhood fears of ghosts have manifested into adult fears—paying bills, keeping our children safe, meeting deadlines, loss of health, and so on. We come to realize that these adult fears are really the ghosts, shadows, and monsters of our childhood in disguise. Fear is fear no matter what shape it takes. Childhood fears can be just as paralyzing as adult fears. Satan wants us to fear because it leads to anger, hate, and a suffering of hopelessness. Fear separates us from God. It leaves us void of faith and hope.

Doctor Cornelius's explanation of how the Telmarines were separated from Cair Paravel because of fear and how they use fear to keep their people from "looking towards Aslan's land and the morning and the eastern end of the world"[43] reflects how Satan fears God and uses fear to alienate others from God. What really stuns me here is how good Satan is at tricking us into believing these lies. Most of our pain and suffering stems from fear, and we don't even realize it.

Tracing Our Fears

Almost all of our frustrations stem from fear. Not surprisingly, this reality has also come from a story. If you have watched the *Star Wars* movies, you will remember the conversation about fear between Yoda and young Anakin. Yoda senses great fear in Anakin and encourages him to let go of his fears. He wisely tells Anakin that fear leads to anger, anger leads to hate, and hate leads to much suffering. This seems quite true. Whenever I am anxious and upset, I can always trace it back to some sort of fear.

Anakin's fear eventually leads him to an angry rage that leaves him suffering alone in a dark hopelessness. Like Nikabrik, his fear leads him on a path to the dark side. We all have this battle. To win our battle against evil, as Lewis advises and shows us in Narnia, we must conquer our fears.

Finding Purpose

What did you fear as a child?

What do you fear now?

Trace back one of your frustrations (suffering, hate, anger, fear). What fear must you conquer to overcome that frustration?

What is your greatest fear?

How does it leave you hopeless and cut you off from God?

When has the Holy Spirit helped you overcome fear and helped you stay strong in the midst of fearful anger and accusations?

Finding Scripture

In Matthew 14:22–33, we see Peter display the same struggle with fear that Lewis discusses and personifies in *Mere Christianity* and *Prince Caspian*. While Jesus is on a mountain praying, the disciples wait out a windy storm on a boat. During the night as the storm still wages, the disciples see him approach, walking on the water. They yell out in terror and wonder if he is a ghost. At once, Jesus tells them to take courage and to not be afraid. Peter tells the figure approaching to prove that he is Jesus by having him also walk on water. He then gets out of the boat and walks on water to Jesus! However, as the winds of the storm increase in strength he becomes fearful, loses faith, and begins to sink. He cries out to Jesus for help, and Jesus stretches out his arm and admonishes Peter's doubt and lack of faith.

Again, do you not see yourself in this story? The apostles' fear a ghost as Caspian did while speaking to Doctor Cornelius. Peter loses faith when the challenge becomes more frightening, as Susan also did. Are not we the same? Do we not allow childish fears to keep us from Jesus? When we start out in faith on the right track, don't we also eventually begin to sink?

Yet, we also receive hope in this story. As soon as Peter cries out for help, Jesus stretches out his hand and pulls Peter back to safety. We also can ask for help. We may not have a horn like Caspian, but we do have prayer. When we feel our faith begin to crumble out of fear, we can pray for Jesus to reach out his hand and pull us back to safety.

Suggested Scripture Reading and Reflections

Read Matthew 14:22–33 and look for yourself in the actions of the disciples.

What are your biggest fears and worries?

When has fear kept you from God?

When have you started out walking on water but then found yourself sinking as the waters became rough?

When has Jesus stretched out his hand to rescue you?

Second Coming

Reflections on Lewis with Caspian

In the Midst of Turmoil

*W*hile watching chaos break out after Peter won his battle with Miraz, it seems that Lewis was calling us to reflect on how the end times are described in the Bible. These suspicions are validated when the enemy looks to the wood as the Old Narnians begin to win and scream, "The end of the world."[44]

Now in our country's history with fighting a war against terrorism, various tragedies, and recovering from assorted natural disasters, many express a fear that the end is near. Countless generations have felt this way before. However, there is a sense of hope in knowing that one day the evil of this world will pass away and those who have believed in and followed Christ will be uplifted and freed from the pain and suffering.

How All Were Very Busy

Do you not constantly hear tales of busyness from those around you? Do you not often tell others about how busy you are? Obviously times have not changed from Lewis's days. He chooses this chapter title to get us to look at our own busyness and gently reminds us not to despair in our busyness, for one day it will be interrupted and brought to an end.

Usually Jesus's second coming is depicted and described with such frightening images that most of us dread it. In reality, we should look forward to it. Those of us who are vigilantly doing Christ's work here on earth will find relief, comfort, and great celebration.

Lewis intentionally shows a very compassionate, loving, and playful Aslan in this chapter in order to make us rethink our current feelings of the second coming of Christ. Aslan begins the day by telling Lucy and Susan, "We will make a Holiday." He then asks them to climb on his back, which they do with great joy. Together they are described as "rushing, leaping, and turning somersaults" with the other "beasts frisking round them."[45] Lewis helps us to see that Christ's second coming may actually be seen as having fun.

Personal Ponderings

Freed from Suffering and Oppression

Following Aslan to visit those who were in the midst of busyness, one watches with intrigue and takes comfort in observing those who Aslan visited and freed from pain and suffering. Again, we see that our times have not changed much from Lewis's times. Aslan first visits a little girl named Gwendolyn who is being bullied and abused in school by her teacher Miss Prizzle. Gwendolyn seeks an education that engages her and meets the needs of her imagination. Unfortunately, Miss Prizzle teaches Gwendolyn a "dull" history that is "less true than the most exciting adventure story."[46] Gwendolyn is like many of students today who are being labeled as learning disabled because they do not fit the mold of the cookie cutter kids' education demands. Clearly, Lewis is commenting here on the inadequacies of education and seeing the treatment of students who buck the system as immoral. Gwendolyn is freed and taken to the party, while Miss Prizzle runs off screaming. It is also interesting to note that Aslan calls

Gwendolyn "sweetheart."[47] With Aslan's words, Lewis pushes us to see that Christ will not only rescue us, but he will call us to join him with intimacy and love; a striking contrast from how we are treated by this world.

Lewis also amazes us when he has Aslan remember to free the dogs, donkeys, horses, and other animals. Some humans treat such creatures inhumanely and abuse them. The recent accounts of football player Michael Vick's involvement with dog fighting are a testament to this. Lewis wants us to reflect on how these creatures are also God's creatures. In the second coming, Lewis believes that they also will be uplifted and freed from their suffering. Their oppressors will be left behind.

Tears welled in my eyes as I read about the boy who was being beaten. Lewis reminds the abused children that Jesus will turn their tears of sorrow to laughter. They can find hope in knowing that Jesus will come to their rescue and take them to a place where they will rejoice and be free from abuse and suffering.

Hope for All

Teachers may find hope in Lewis's attention to the teacher who continues to teach compassionately to apathetic, ill-mannered, and nonappreciative students. Aslan recognized her efforts and freed her from the schoolhouse. One can laugh at Lewis's turning the horrid students into pigs. Surely, many educators find hope and justice in this scene.

Likewise, those who are suffering with health issues and caring for those who are ill will find great hope in Aslan's visit to Bachus and her mother. Lewis not only has Aslan compassionately cure her of her illness, but he also turns their well water into "the richest wine, red as redcurrant jelly, smooth as oil, strong as beef, warming as tea, cool as dew."[48] With this allusion, Lewis sends us to other scripture stories of hope: the woman at the well and Jesus's turning water into wine at Cana. Additionally, Lewis reminds us that one of our greatest sources of hope and strength is Christ's presence in his body and blood in the Holy Eucharist. At the Last Supper, Jesus turned an ordinary drink into his life-giving blood that will make us whole and strong. Lewis reminds us here that there is healing in Jesus's blood.

Finding Purpose

Whom did you most relate with in the chapter?
Why?
If Jesus came today, what would he find you busy doing?
From what would his coming free you?
How does looking toward Jesus's coming give you hope?

Finding Scripture

Lewis alludes to the end times in *Prince Caspian* as a way to help us reflect on our own readiness. What will we be busy doing when Jesus returns? Jesus has told us that we will not know the day nor the hour of his second coming, but he advises us to be always prepared, for it will come like a thief in the night.

In Matthew 25:1–13, Jesus uses a parable of ten brides-maids who await a groom. Those who have extra oil for their lamps are prepared and waiting when the groom arrives, while those who did not bring extra oil leave to find some and miss the arrival of the groom. The message is clear. Stay spiritually awake and vigilant, so we are ready when Jesus comes to rescue us.

> ## Suggested Scripture Reading and Reflections
>
> Read Matthew 25:1–13 and reflect on what Jesus may be teaching us.
>
> What differentiates the five wise virgins from the foolish ones?
> What are we to do to be wise?
> What do the lamps represent?
> What must we use for the oil?
> How can we be sure to have enough oil?
> How can we stay awake?
> How does this parable offer us hope?

The Final Battle

Reflections on Lewis with Caspian

Hope in the Midst of Adversity

*W*atching the battle between Peter and Miraz unfold, Peter's honor and nobility impresses us. Even when his wrist is hurt and Edmund fears that Peter may not win, Peter bravely holds on to hope and nobly thinks of others first. He tells Edmund, "I have a chance if I can keep him on the hop….Give my love to—to everyone at home, Ed, if he gets me." During a battle that Peter describes to us as "very tough," we don't hear words of anger or hate. Why? Because Peter holds on to hope and does not fear.[49]

Our society that upholds and respects leaders and celebrities who lash out in times of adversity seems to perpetuate situational ethics that deem it acceptable to curse, react violently, and express hatred when trouble comes our way. We are taught to let our situation determine our actions. In Peter's battle, Lewis gives a different role model. Through Peter, we see Christ's teachings. Even in the midst of his death, Christ offered forgiveness and love to his enemies. He did not curse them; he forgave them. Like Peter, even while facing death, Jesus reached out in love to his family. He did not worry about himself but asked John to care for his mother.

Brother Supporting Brother

Edmund's care and support for his brother during the battle is also touching. In fact, it reminds us of the scripture that warns of how brothers will turn on each other in the final battle of our faith. Lewis is trying to give us a counter example here. One can almost envision him screaming aloud: "See. It does not have to be that way in the end. It does not have to be brother against brother and mother against daughter. Reach out in love to one another. Do not fear. Stand strong and hope!"

Can you hear him also? I am ashamed to think of the many times I have not reached out in love. I seem to get frustrated easily and lash out at the very ones I love the most. Haven't you done the same?

Peter's enemy learns the result of his vengeful lashing, for it is when "Miraz is angry" that he trips "on a tussock" and goes "down." Metaphorically, Lewis shows us that "anger is our downfall." We are called to act as noble sons and daughters of God, even when facing death in battle. Peter steps back when he sees Miraz fall. He doesn't take advantage of the moment. Instead, he acts "like a High King" and waits for Miraz "to rise." Peter's noble character frustrates Edmund at first, but with thought and wisdom he understands "it is what Aslan would like."[50]

Lewis shows us here that acting with nobility in the midst of battle is also what "God would like." These acts of nobility come from hope and love; we have hope that acting in love will help us to win out in the end. God is love, and it is love that will lead us to win our final battles of faith. Love allowed Christ to resurrect and rise from death; love will keep us from lashing out at one another in the end. Hope leads us and love will unite us and allow us to triumph and find Christ even amidst our adversaries.

Personal Ponderings

Battles of a Parent

Some of my most trying battles are as a parent. Patience and understanding, love and forgiveness need to be learned daily. And Satan seems to try us when we are at our weakest moments.

You may recall times when children's actions, which are often playful in nature, became antagonizing and provoked negative reactions. These moments can leave us feeling hopeless—to gain control and order we sternly utter harsh words of rebuke, especially if their actions are causing us to have a headache. When we are not feeling well physically, our patience becomes even less, and we act in ways that are not always loving. In these battles, we may not do as well as Peter.

In these trying times, when we find ourselves at our weakest moments, our only saving grace may be prayer. During difficult situations like these, have you not found yourself folding your hands and praying for the strength, courage, and patience needed? And during spiritual timeouts, do you not find God calming you? Does he not help you find just the right words and actions to redirect the situation?

Parents know that discipline is never easy. Asking for forgiveness for lost patience, for words that never should have been spoken, and for actions that occurred from frustration at a moment of weakness are also not easy, but they may give way to family reconciliation and an expression of love.

Clearly, leading with love and hope wins more battles than anger and frustration. Why is it so hard to remember that, even after we have witnessed and experienced it?

Finding Purpose

When have you lost hope and lashed out in anger and frustration at your loved ones?

How has God given you hope in times of despair?

When has love helped you redirect your failings and find God?

What are your toughest spiritual battles?

How can you fight with courage and nobility?

Finding Scripture

Jesus gives us the best example of loving our enemies and acting with nobility when facing frustration, weakness, anger, hostility, and enemies. In the Garden of Gethsemane, he turns to prayer in a moment of weakness while asking for God's will to be done. Then when the chief priests come to take Jesus away, one of the disciples draws his sword and cuts off one of the high priest's ears.

Jesus criticizes the disciple's conduct and tells him to put his sword away. He tells him and us that those who use and rely on the sword will die by it. Jesus peacefully accepts his death and resurrection, remarkably praying to God for the forgiveness of his persecutors. How many of us could find the mercy and nobility to love our enemies as they taunt us, spit on us, and kill us? Yet, that is what we are called to do.

Suggested Scripture Reading and Reflections

Read Matthew 26:36—27:54 and note how Jesus acts toward his persecutors.

How does Jesus act toward his persecutors?

What qualities did you notice about him in reading this scripture passage? Make a list.

What would have been the result if Jesus fought back with anger and hostility?

When have you lashed out in anger?

What was the result?

When have you reached out with love?

What was the result?

How can you imitate the qualities Jesus displayed the next time you are tempted to lash out in anger?

Why does love result in more hope than anger?

What is the result of anger?

Section Three
Learning to Love

And now faith, hope, and love abide, these three;
and the greatest of these is love.
1 Corinthians 13:13

Fear, Awe, and Love

Reflections on Lewis with Caspian

*A*s Christians, we are given a confusing mix of how we are to feel about God. Scripture teaches us that we are to have fear, awe, and love for God. But what does that really mean? Lewis tells us that awe comes quite naturally when we look at the great universe that God has created. In this sense, he seems a "great artist" who has created a "beautiful place." Yet when we look at the moral law that God has handed down to us, we have no grounds to find God as "indulgent, soft, or sympathetic"—for there is "nothing indulgent about the moral law. It is as hard as nails."[1]

In giving us this moral law to follow, we are expected "to do the straight thing and it does not seem to care how painful, or dangerous, or difficult it is to do."[2] The God we meet here is definitely not "soft." We may have much fear about what we are called to do and what will result if we do not follow. So our awe of God naturally brings us to him. We are attracted to his goodness and long to be in his presence. However, at the same time, knowing God means following him, and his tasks are never easy. In fact, they cause us a great deal of challenge at times. Lewis describes this well when he says: "God is the only comfort, He is also the supreme terror: the thing we most need and the thing we most want to hide from."[3] He goes on to personify these seemingly paradoxical emotions in the Narnia characters' feelings toward Aslan.

In the character of Lucy, Lewis gives us a glimpse of the awe and excitement we feel in loving God. As she hears her name called by Aslan (even though she doesn't from the start consciously recognize his name), Lewis tells us that "she sat up with trembling but not with fear."[4] As she walks on toward the voice, we are given awe-inspiring descriptions of nature that appears to have come to life. The nature connects us to the awe we feel in God's creation.

As she gets nearer to Aslan, she "felt her own feet wanting to dance," and she gives in to the urge as she "went fearlessly, dancing herself as she leapt." When she finally sees Aslan, Lewis describes the encounter as "oh joy!" and Lucy "never stopped to think if he was a friendly lion or not. She rushed to him" because "she felt her heart would burst if she lost a moment." She then proceeds to bury herself in his mane, "kissing him and putting her arms as far round his neck as she could."[5] Clearly, in this scene, Lewis shows us our awe-inspired love of God. For don't we also have this urge deep in our souls to run to God and bury ourselves in his arms?

Fear keeps us from fully rejoicing in the awesomeness of God's love. Lewis also shows us this as Lucy's siblings and Trumpkin find Aslan. When they realize that Lucy was right and reflect on how awful they had treated her and how their actions had kept them from Aslan, they see Aslan somewhat differently than Lucy did. They do not leap into his mane with joy. Their guilt causes them to fear Aslan. For they know the greatness of Aslan and have remorse in not following him from the start. Lewis tells us that as they stood looking at the "majestic" lion "they felt as glad as anyone can who feels afraid, and as afraid as anyone who feels glad."[6] Here do we not find the same paradox that Lewis mentioned in *Mere Christianity*? "God is the only comfort, He is also the supreme terror: the thing we most need and the thing we most want to hide from" (see note 2). The children find comfort in finding Aslan because only he can help them, yet they want to hide because of the shame they feel for their actions. Thus, they act as they should and we should. They fall to their knees and say, "I'm sorry."

Personal Ponderings

Most of us would probably like to say that we approach God as Lucy did, but we are most like the others. Perhaps a closer look at how we approach God in the sacraments will show how we really do approach him. For example, how do you feel as you look at Jesus in the Eucharist, knowing that he died for your sins and is right there before you for you to receive? Do you rush to him? Or do you guiltily feel the need to look away because you are not worthy? I must admit that I find myself humbled and feeling very unworthy in his presence. I do not love him any less, but I fear that I do not deserve his love because I know that I do not always live up to his expectations.

The sacrament of reconciliation is another occasion where we encounter the loving forgiveness of God. Will any priest tell you that parishioners are rushing through the doors to get in line in front of the confessional? Why? As one might guess, our fear keeps us away. We fear that we are not worthy to be forgiven. We wonder what the priest will think. We do not want to admit that we have done wrong. All of these things keep us from God. This fear can be a deterrent. However, it is a healthy fear that reminds us that God expects great things from us and leads us to him. For as Lewis describes the paradox, we long to be with God. We long to please him, and we can only find that happiness in serving him, no matter how challenging and difficult his calling might be.

Another place we might find a better understanding of this mix of fear and awe is in *The Wizard of Oz*. Dorothy, the Lion, the Scarecrow, and the Tin Man all sought out the Wizard because they knew he was the only one who could help them. When they arrived to visit the Wizard, they became frightened and overcome with awe. They were almost too afraid to knock on the door and take their requests to him. When they do enter, they work very hard to make themselves presentable. Their desire to look their best is out of a sense of respect and reverence.

Isn't this the same type of feeling we have for God? Do we not also fear that we will not be presentable to him? The difference is that God really can help us and is worthy of our awe, unlike the Wizard.

Finding Purpose

When have you been in awe of God's presence?

When have you felt a fear of God?

How does the paradoxical combination of fear and awe lead you to love God?

When have you felt the need to bury yourself in God's arms?

What kept you from doing so?

Finding Scripture

In the Gospel of John, Peter helps us to understand how our love for God contains both fear and awe. In him, we can also see that even when we sin we can rush out to meet God with joy. All four Gospels tell of how Jesus foretold that Peter would deny him, how Peter did deny him three times as predicted, and how he wept bitterly afterward. However, only the Gospel of John lets us see Jesus and Peter interact after Jesus's resurrection.

Most of us would probably expect Peter to fear Jesus and want to hide from him because he did deny him as Jesus foretold. However, John tells us that Peter leapt out of the boat and swam to meet Jesus on the shore. He also shared a meal with Jesus. Nowhere does it show that Peter retreated from or feared Jesus's presence. As Lucy rejoiced at the sight of Aslan, Peter leapt at the sight of Jesus.

Then, while sharing a meal, Jesus asks Peter three times if he loves him. Peter proclaims his love all three times, and each time Jesus gives him a task. Here Jesus shows Peter how he can make up for denying him. Jesus calls him to feed and tend to his sheep. Here we see that not only does Jesus forgive us if we are sorry, but we can show our love for him by taking care of our fellow Christians. In loving each other, we love God. Although we do need to fear denying God with our sins, Peter shows us that we can still return to God with joy and love. However, God will not lessen our load. Peter is told here that he will face a death similar to Jesus because of his service to God.

Suggested Scripture Reading and Reflections

Read John 13:31–38 and reflect on Peter's interaction with Jesus.

How would you describe Peter's feelings for Jesus in this scene?

Why is he so sure that he will not deny Jesus?

When have you acted this way?

Why do you think Peter's denial follows Jesus's commandment of love?

Why is the placement significant?

Read John 18:15–27 about Peter's denial of Jesus.

Why does Peter deny Jesus?

Would you have done the same?

How does he feel after the cock crowed?

When have you felt this way?

Read John 21:1–19 about Peter rejoicing in Jesus's return. This passage gives us hope so that we can also rush to Jesus, even after we have sinned.

Peter did not see Jesus at first. What do you need to do to see God's presence among you?

What boat would you need to jump out of to meet Jesus on the shore?

How is God asking you to love him and serve him?

What part of this call is challenging and frightening?

How will you meet this calling?

Too Much Honor

Reflections on Lewis with Caspian

*I*n *Surprised by Joy,* Lewis tells us about the many abuses he suffered by the education system. In his autobiography, we recognize a school class system where the strong and older students beat up and take advantage of the younger, smaller, and weaker children. Lewis tells us about some moments where these abuses made him want to die. Many of us have had at least one experience with this.

He also tells us that these experiences led him to become what he called a prig or a snob. In an attempt to become stronger and less abused, he looked up to a fellow student who he names Pogo. He tells us that under the direction of this boy he lost his "certain humble and childlike and self-forgetful qualities," as he "began to labor very hard to make [him]self into a fop, a cad, and a snob."[7] This he believes was part of his downfall away from God.

We get another glimpse of this in the character of Reepicheep when he puts the utmost importance on his tail. After Lucy used her bottle of ointment to heal Reepicheep's many wounds, he jumps up, grabs his hilt, and begins to bow before Aslan to offer his service. However, as he realizes that his tail is no longer attached, he stops and loses his confidence. He tells Aslan that he is "confounded" and apologizes for appearing in such an "unseemly fashion." While he realizes that he is still able to function and serve without his tail, he is very upset because he believes the tail to be "the honour and glory of a mouse." That is when Aslan responds: "I have sometimes wondered friend if you do not think too much about your honour."[8] Lewis appears to be addressing himself and us here. Surely when Lewis relied on his intellect and became what he describes a priggish snob, he was thinking too much of his honor.

Have we not also been guilty of the same? Don't we also spend too much time obsessing about the little unnecessary things that we don't have and value ourselves accordingly? Lewis shows us here that God only asks that we serve him with what we are given. Society has different values than God. Whereas society focuses on outward appearances and possessions, God looks inward and only asks that we serve him with the gifts he has given us.

Personal Ponderings

It seems that most of our concerns and worries over what we have and do not have occurs in times of transitions. For example, think back to your first day of high school. How much thought did you put into your clothes, hair, and complexion? Did you make judgments about yourself based on your appearance and belongings? Didn't you assume others would assess you the same?

We may remember falsely thinking that our external appearance would determine popularity. Status is often determined by friends, and of course, friends are gained by appearance. People want to be around other people who feel confident about themselves, not around someone self-conscious of his or her appearance. When you are yourself, you naturally attract others who are like you and want to be around you. In other words, you use what God has given you with confidence.

Beginning a new job or career can also cause those same feelings of insecurity. You want to look your best and act your best. You compare yourself to everyone else around you and assume you are not as good. You pay attention to what they are wearing and what they are talking about so that you can be like everyone else. However, this again only sets us up for failure. We are hired because of who we are and what we have. Although we do need to fit in, we don't do this by pretending to be who we are not or by obsessing over what we don't have. We fit in by being ourselves and successfully using the abilities we have been given.

As parents see their children entering the teenage years, they are reminded about how they saw themselves as adolescents. They may cringe at remembering how much they obsessed over outward appearances and the opinions of their peers. If we only knew then what we know now! But no matter how we try to tell our teenagers what we have learned, those lessons only come with experience and maturity. God must feel the same way watching us grow and mature in our faith.

Sometimes we can cause others pain and suffering by longing for honor. This is called pride—one of the deadly sins. One cannot help but think about the role that pride played in the recent Virginia Tech shootings. The student who openly fired on his classmates and teachers obviously was seeking to be noticed. In his videotape, writings, and tattoos, he makes it clear that he did not feel respected or honored by others. As disturbing as his actions and messages were, they revealed that he sought some sort of vindication, retribution, and honor. He even went so far as to describe his act as service to God. Painfully, this shows us how we can obsess too much about our honor or lack thereof. In this case, pride became deadly in a physical and spiritual sense. Yet, it also shows us we need to respect one another so that we never make someone feel like an outcast. In our own prideful actions and obsessions with honor, we may end up stripping someone else of their honor.

Jesus told us to love our neighbor as ourselves. Wisely, Lewis explains that this really has little to do with affection. Rather it has to do with will. We must learn to see others and treat others as we do ourselves. About this, he says: "Do not waste time bothering whether you 'love' your neighbor; act as if you did." He then goes on to explain this further in noting that behaving as you love someone usually brings you to feel more fondly toward that person. Whereas if you continue to injure someone you dislike, you will grow to hate that person. And in being kind toward others, we must also be careful not to make a big deal about it or expect gratitude. For as Lewis recognizes and reminds us: "People are not fools: they have a quick eye for anything like showing off, or patronage."[9]

Unfortunately, the young man at Virginia Tech was not treated kindly and likewise did not treat others kindly. It created a vicious cycle that resulted in a tragedy that affected us all.

Lewis uses Reepicheep's fellow mouse friends to give us a glimpse of what it means to love others as ourselves. They openly volunteer to have their tails removed so that Reepicheep will feel better about himself. They willingly offer to give up their own prized possession for the sake of a fellow mouse. Aslan, in recognizing their kindness and love, replaces Reepicheep's tail—his honor. Would you be able to do the same? Would it matter who the person was? In these scenes, Lewis calls us to reflect on these questions.

Finding Purpose

What do you obsess most over? Why?

What outward appearances do you judge yourself by? Others?

How could you let go of these obsessions?

What inner talents and gifts has God given you to use?

How could you become more accepting of yourself? Others?

How well do you do in loving your neighbor?

How can you improve on this?

Finding Scripture

In the book of Genesis, we see how pride plays out in the story of Joseph and his brothers. Joseph, the favored son of Jacob, goes to great lengths to display his talents and gifts. Jacob gives Joseph a long tunic, which Joseph proudly wears and outwardly reminds his brothers that he is the favored son. Additionally, Joseph does not hesitate to share his dreams with his brothers. The problem is that in his dreams he is always above them. His brothers grow jealous and eventually sell him into slavery.

When I was younger, I use to feel very sorry for Joseph. But now I can see where Joseph may have been flaunting his favoritism to his brothers. As the youngest, he sought respect and honor. He wanted to be one of them and unwisely thought that his coat and dreams may gain him the respect and prestige he desired.

Two lessons seem to emerge from this story. God gives us gifts but he does not want us to flaunt them with a great deal of pride. Joseph could have kept his dreams and coat to himself or perhaps shared and used them more humbly. In flaunting his favoritism and dreams, he may have contributed to the personal difficulties he endured of losing his family and spending many years in slavery.

The second lesson comes from the brothers. They had no need to compare themselves to Joseph. In comparing themselves, they became jealous and overlooked the gifts that they had. Jealousy is a deadly sin, and it caused their father, Joseph, and themselves much unnecessary grief and suffering. Their actions brought death to their family. They lost their own honor. Ironically, they actualized their own fears, as their brother's dreams became a reality. However, Joseph learns from his actions and humbly forgives and helps his brothers. He learns to share his gifts and use them to help others rather than to flaunt them.

Suggested Scripture Reading and Reflections

Read chapters 37, 42, and 43 from Genesis and note how Joseph changes in how he relates to his brothers.

How would you describe the young Joseph?

The grown Joseph?

When have you felt like the brothers did toward the young Joseph: envious or angered toward someone who has more than you do?

How did you act toward this person?

When have you acted like the young Joseph?

How did others react?

How could you grow to become more like the adult Joseph?

Nature Comes to Life

Reflections on Lewis with Caspian

*A*s indicated in section 1, Lewis admits in *Surprised by Joy* that nature awakened longings in him.[10] He later realized these longings as his "love of God." In fact, he even concludes that without these stirrings, he would never have become aware of "the huge areas of what" he came to recognize as love of God. In other words, Lewis found nature to stir him and lead him to God. He saw nature as a reflection and force through which God worked. However, he also made it very clear that he did not believe that nature could teach. He found those who looked to nature for answers as foolish and believed that in that sense nature might even lead to a religion of its own—where we love nature rather than God.[11] Although this may seem confusing, he beautifully illustrates his meaning with Lucy.

In the scene described earlier, where Lucy hears Aslan's call, Lewis shows that nature contributes to Lucy's calling and awakening. As Aslan calls her from her out "of the deepest sleep you can imagine," the "moon was so bright that the whole forest landscape around her was almost as clear as day." As she tries to make sense of what is going on, she walks toward the trees that seem to also be walking. As she sees the trees begin to dance, she also begins to dance. Yet, Lewis is careful here to tell us that while nature seemed to be mirroring and stirring Lucy's emotions, "she was only half interested in them. She wanted to get beyond them to something else; it was from beyond them that the dear voice had called."[12]

Here we get a sense of what Lewis's awakening must have been like and what he means when he says that nature can stir us and help us to recognize our love for God. Nature stirs Lucy and causes her joy and excitement to build as it also points to the direction of Aslan. She knows that nature is not the focus and Aslan is what exists beyond nature.

Lewis exemplifies his beliefs here that nature should not be our focus. We do not find God in nature itself, but it can direct us, lead us, and stir us. If we focus solely on nature rather than what is beyond it, we may never find God.

Personal Ponderings

Reading this scene may remind you of times when you have walked alone through the woods and felt as though the trees were alive. As the wind blew them, the leaves looked as though they were dancing and singing with each other. The rays of sunlight also appeared to clothe them in bright yellow. Then following the path of rays, were your eyes directed upward toward the heavens? A warm joy may have filled you as you felt the presence of God. The birds and the squirrels also seemed to feel the presence as they sang, chattered, and basked in the glorious surroundings. Have you ever experienced this?

Lewis's and Lucy's stirrings seem to reflect this type of experience. In those moments when nature surrounds you, nothing else seems to matter. No thoughts of money, food, clothes, or other worldly matters enter into your thoughts. God calls; nature then leads and creates the most peaceful atmosphere to allow you to just bask in God's glory and love.

The book and recent movie *Bridge to Terabithia* is another example of finding refuge in nature. The main characters, Jesse and Leslie, escape from life—bullies, poverty, detached parents, school. There they release their inner longings. The movie also brilliantly animates the forest to depict their imaginative play where nature comes to life. In the story, nature leads them to discover their God-given gifts: Jesse draws and Leslie writes. They also find friendship.

Sometimes it is tempting to stay just there, away from the rest of the world. Indeed some have done this, like Henry David Thoreau did at Walden. However, wouldn't that be selfish? How can we do God's work if we never return? Jesus also sought peace, rest, and solitude in nature and the desert, but he always returned to God's work. And so must we.

Bridge to Terabithia also teaches this important lesson. Leslie becomes so obsessed with Terabithia that she takes an unnecessary risk. She goes alone when the stream is too high to cross. In crossing with the rope, it breaks, and she drowns in the rising water. In focusing too much on the stirrings and delight of Terabithia, she wanders out alone and puts herself in danger. The result is deadly. Could this not also happen to us, both physically and spiritually? While nature may lead us to God, we must be careful not to let it consume us. As Lewis advises, we must, like Lucy, realize what we are really looking for is the voice beyond it.

Finding Purpose

What in nature has allowed you to find God?
What feelings were stirred in you?
What did you discover there?
When has nature become a distraction or obsession?
How did you find your way back?
Why do we seek to escape in nature?
How can we keep a healthy balance?

Finding Scripture

The story about the Garden of Eden offers the same lesson for us. Adam and Eve live in harmony with nature and God. God gives to humanity all of the plants, fruit, and creatures. Nature is a gift to us from God. It is intended to nourish and reflect his goodness and love. Yet, humanity grows to focus on it alone as a source of truth and knowledge. In eating the forbidden fruit from the tree of the knowledge of good and evil and attempting to become God, humanity sins and undergoes a death, a separation from God. Here we see that nature is not to be looked at as an end in itself, but rather as a reflection of God's love, goodness, and glory. In focusing on nature and not its source, we find separation, sin, and death. In Genesis 2:17, God warns us that if we eat from the tree of knowledge we will die. This warning should be understood as a spiritual death. In forgetting about God and focusing only on nature as a source of truth and knowledge, we separate ourselves from God.

Suggested Scripture Reading and Reflections

Read Genesis 2—3 and reflect on humanity's relationship with nature before and after the fall and how it affects our relationship with God.

How does our society seek answers from nature?
How does this separate and distance us from God?
In what ways does science compete with God?
How can science and God be brought into a healthy relationship?
When have you found a stirring or longing in nature?
How did it lead you to God?

Kindred Spirits

Reflections on Lewis with Caspian

*L*ewis experienced death at an early age. In his autobiography, he tells us that when he was still a young boy, cancer took his mother away from him. He describes her death as what some might consider his "first religious experience." He prayed fervently and faithfully to God that she might be healed. However, he does not consider it a religious experience because he "approached God...without love, without awe, even without fear." Looking back, he realizes that he thought of God "merely as a magician." With the loss of his mother, "all that was tranquil and reliable, disappeared."[13]

However, we see that he later found hope in being reunited with loved ones in an afterlife. Shortly before his own death, he writes in a letter to Arthur Greeves of his sadness in knowing that they will "never meet again in this life,"[14] which surely shows his faith that they will meet again in another life. He also gives us a glimpse of what it might be like to be reunited with our own loved ones when Caspian is reunited with his childhood nurse.

After the final battle when Lucy and Susan return with Aslan, we see the old woman who Aslan made slip from his back and run to Caspian with joy. As the two embrace one another, we discover that she is Caspian's old nurse.[15] In this short scene, Lewis gives us hope. One day, we will be reunited with our own kindred spirits.

Personal Ponderings

One cannot imagine the grief and horror that Lewis experienced as he was forced to look at his dead mother and tell her goodbye. The biggest fear for many children is that their parents will die while they are young.

I remember praying every night that God would not take my parents from me. Like Lewis, I see that I was not approaching God as I should. In my pleadings, I realize now that I was not approaching him with the love, awe, and fear he deserves. Irreverently, I saw him more as a controlling puppeteer. Most children do see God as controlling and powerful.

The fear of losing one's parents seems to show a lack of spiritual maturity. Focusing primarily on this transient, temporal world and not eternity with God, many are looking at this present earthly life as better and not trusting that God would take care of our future needs. This is a struggle we constantly face. Even with the scripture reminders about how to live our lives and the promise of the resurrection, we just do not seem to get it. The messages of this world convince us to think primarily in terms of the present moment—the here and now. So when a loved one dies, our world is rocked. We focus on our loss and not on the new and better world that our loved one has entered. We may even forget that we will one day be reunited.

Many of us have watched loved ones enter nursing homes. As their savings become drained, they must sell off possessions to pay the bills. They feel remorse because they have no legacy to leave behind. When they die, we must watch the rest of their worldly treasures be auctioned off to strangers. Even more troubling are the family fights over the deceased's possessions. Each member feels that one has a right to certain heirlooms and treasures of the estate that are not stipulated in the will.

However, we need to realize that each one of us owns our own memories. It is not about the worldly objects lying all around. The love that had been shared with us and the memories that lived in our hearts will always be part of us. It is about the relationships we formed with them. The moments that we had secretly stored away and pull out every once and awhile to remember. Those will always live inside us; they have transformed us and made us what we are. One day, we will meet again. But for now, they must live in our hearts.

Finding Purpose

When have you struggled with letting go of a loved one?
Why is death so hard for us?
Why is it so hard for us to fathom another life after this?
Why do we get so attached to this world?
How can we be more spiritually focused?
How has Jesus's resurrection changed us?

Finding Scripture

In John 11, we read about the death of Lazarus, the brother of Martha and Mary, who was a close friend of Jesus. When he hears of Lazarus's illness, Jesus consciously waits for two days to pass before he visits him. It is not until Lazarus has died that Jesus arrives in Bethany. He tells us that Lazarus must suffer and die so that others may come to believe.

Martha runs out to greet Jesus as he approaches. She is upset and wonders why Jesus did not do anything to prevent Lazarus from dying. However, she does proclaim her faith in Jesus and that she knows Lazarus will rise in the afterlife and that she will one day see him again there. More significantly, she displays a faith that God will give Jesus anything that he asks. He tells us that those who truly believe in him will never die because he is the resurrection and the life.

When Mary approaches Jesus, she is much more distraught over the death of her brother. Weeping, she asks Jesus why he did not save Lazarus from death. Her weeping also brings Jesus to weep. Here we see the human side of Jesus. He shows compassion. He grieves with us and shares our pain and suffering. He weeps for us here, for our loss, and for our lack of faith.

With tears still on his face, Jesus calls Lazarus from the tomb of death. Lazarus then rises and comes out of the tomb full of life. Mary, Martha, and Lazarus are reunited. Scripture is very clear here. Jesus will raise all of us who believe in him to eternal life. We will not die, and we will be reunited with the ones we love.

Lewis finally came to understand fully this toward the end of his life. In a letter to Arthur Greeves, he tells him that he had peacefully fallen into a coma only to be pulled back to life from it. Of the experience, he says, "Poor Lazarus!"—which shows a faith and desire to be in the afterlife. In being pulled back, both Lazarus and Lewis were brought back to a less than perfect life. Yet, he finishes with confidence that "God knows best."[16]

Suggested Scripture Reading and Reflections

Read John 11 and spend some time thinking about how Jesus changed our lives with his resurrection.

When have you felt like Martha? Mary?
Why did Jesus weep?
What does his emotion mean for you personally?
Who are you most anxious to be reunited with?

Like a Bumbling Bear

Reflections of Lewis with Caspian

C. S. Lewis was very close to his brother Warren. In *Surprised by Joy*, we hear how both of them turned to each other for companionship when their mother died. After Warren went away to school, Lewis waited eagerly at the end of each term for his older brother to return home for a visit.

However, in *They Stand Together,* we see another side of Warren. In the introduction and in the letters, we find that Warren struggled with alcoholism throughout most of his life. Sometimes he would be in such a drunken stupor, he would be forced to seek refuge in a convent. Many who knew Warren probably wondered what virtue his brother may have seen in him.

In fact, Lewis's final letter to Greeves indicates that Lewis felt much frustration toward Warren. He had not responded to any letters regarding Lewis's coma and condition. He felt abandoned from his brother and tells Greeves, "Warren, meanwhile, has completely deserted me." However, the key word here is *meanwhile,* for it shows some hope (even though little) that Warren will still come to his side.[17]

Lewis's hope waned and Warren's virtue proved to be true. Warren did come to his brother's bedside to care for him in his final days. He responded to mail and provided him care and comfort. In the end, it was just the two brothers, Warren and Lewis, together. In the introduction of *Letters of C. S. Lewis,* Warren tells us in his own words that in the final days before his brother's death:

> [We] could turn for comfort only to each other. The wheel had come full circle; once again we were together in the little end room at home, shutting out from our

talk the ever-present knowledge that the holidays were ending, that a new term fraught with unknown possibilities awaited us both.[18]

Here, we learn to see Warren as his brother saw him. His words show us a relationship and bond between the two of them that only they could understand. Clearly, despite Warren's drinking, he was able to step up and cater to the needs of his brother in Lewis's final days.

Lewis knew this also. For when Warren returned, C. S. Lewis wrote to his friend Walter Hooper to tell him that Warren would take care of his needs. Although he loved Hooper dearly and compared not seeing him to a "drawn tooth,"[19] he knew that it was Warren who must be there in the end. Is this not also the case with God? Does he not also see our virtues and trust in them when everyone else only sees our vices?

In *Prince Caspian,* Lewis teaches us this lesson in the character of the eldest Bulgy bear. When he comes forth and asks to serve as one of the marshals for the battle between Peter and Miraz, he argues that "it was always a right of the bears to supply one marshal of the list." Trumpkin, while acknowledging that the bear "is a good creature," fears that the bear will shame them all by sucking on his paws in front of the enemy. Peter looks beyond the bears "paw sucking" and allows him to be marshal because it is his right to serve as marshal.[20]

Although when writing this story Lewis could not possibly have foreseen what would happen in his final days, he might have equated the bear's paw sucking with Warren's drinking habits. Like Peter, he saw Warren deserving respect as his brother, despite his vice, because it was his right. Lewis knew that he must look for the virtues in others, as Jesus did.

Personal Ponderings

In this scene, Lewis gives us a chance to see ourselves on both sides. Like Trumpkin, each of us has judged someone inadequate for a task. Likewise, like the bear, have we not also been judged as inadequate?

In reflecting on Trumpkin, one may see the education system. As the behavior disorder label continues to include more and more students, we see many children feeling cheated of an education. They are entitled to an education that teaches to their specific learning abilities, yet they are judged inadequate for a variety of reasons and shuttled out to a classroom that considers them inferior. Many rebel because they have never felt respected or cared about. They lack confidence, and they feel abused and battered. When no one reaches out to them with love, they lash out in the same manner in which they have been treated. We all lose from this injustice. Like Peter, we must see our children's rights and strengths. We must channel those and look beyond their vices.

We may ask ourselves how we have felt when we have been looked at and judged for only our faults. We all have them. None of us is perfect. We all have strengths and weaknesses. Where would we be if others only saw our faults? We would be in the same situations that many community members find themselves—homeless, friendless, hopeless, suicidal, addicted to substances, in jail, unemployed, divorced, labeled with a disability, and so on. Perhaps some of us are already in one or more of these situations.

To avoid judging ourselves and others, we need to remember that we are all equal in God's eyes. We all have strengths. He calls us to use these for his good. He does not obsess about our faults, nor should we. While we are called to work to better ourselves and should not be arrogant about our gifts, we should not define ourselves by our vices. In a letter to his friend Malcolm, Lewis gives good advice on how to go about this. He says: "I sometimes pray not for self-knowledge in general but for just so much self-knowledge at the moment as I can bear and use at the moment; the little daily dose."[21] For some of us, this daily dose includes a reminder of not to judge others.

The Lion and the Mouse

My daughter recently brought home a version of the Aesop fable, "The Lion and the Mouse." If you recall the story, you will see that it also illustrates this lesson. The lion was resting peacefully when a mouse ran up his tail. Annoyed that the mouse woke him from his nap, the lion contemplated bringing down his large, mighty paw upon the tiny creature. After all, he was larger and the king of the beasts. The mouse was tiny and annoying. What purpose could he serve?

The mouse pleaded with the lion and argued that he may one day be able to help the lion. The lion found his pleadings amusing and decided to let him go.

However, a day did come when the lion needed the mouse's help. The lion found himself trapped in a net by hunters. The mouse happened to be nearby and came to his rescue. He chewed away the net and set the lion free.

There are a couple lessons in this story. As discussed, we all have vices and virtues. The lion in his arrogance did not think the mouse had any value. He judged him to be of little value because of his size. However, the little mouse later saved the lion's life. Because he was patient with the mouse, his life was later saved.

The mouse found his vice in his own mischief. Annoying and awakening the lion endangered his life. Likely, he thought twice before running up a lion's tail. He also learned that his size could be of value. Even though he was small, he could be useful and offer service to others—even big and powerful lions.

Finding Purpose

When have you been like the Bulgy Bear and the mouse? What was the result?

Who has believed in you when others have not?

When have you been like Trumpkin and the lion? What was the result?

When have you focused on someone's God-given abilities and looked beyond that person's faults? What was the result?

What can you do to be less judgmental of others? Yourself?

Finding Scripture

In the Gospel of Luke, Zacchaeus may seem like the Bulgy bear. He is judged inadequate by others because he is a tax collector. However, Jesus sees into his heart and his right of inheritance for he is a descendant of Abraham.

In this story, we see Zacchaeus scamper up into a tree to get a glimpse of Jesus from a distance. Jesus senses his presence and asks him to hurry down for Jesus plans to have dinner in his house that very night. Zacchaeus receives Jesus with joy and proclaims that he will give Jesus half of his possessions and pay those he has extorted from four times what he took from them.

Not surprisingly, the Pharisees looked at Jesus's mingling with Zacchaeus unfavorably. Even the disciples wondered why Jesus would have dinner with such a person. However, Jesus makes it clear that we are all loved and valued by God. Our vices are not God's focus. He loves us for who we are, including our sins. His love is unconditional. In this story, Jesus displays such a love.

Suggested Scripture Reading and Reflections

Read Luke 19:1–10 and note how Zacchaeus is judged, how Zacchaeus reacts to being judged, and the actions of Jesus toward him.

When have you been treated similar to Zacchaeus by the community or society?

How did you react?

When has someone reached out to you like Jesus did to Zacchaeus?

How did you react?

Why do you think Zacchaeus decides to change his ways?

Why does Jesus make note of the fact that Zacchaeus is a descendant of Abraham?

How does this speak to us today?

How does this story speak of unconditional love?

Beyond Blame

Reflections on Lewis with Caspian

Forgive and Forget

Most of us have become so good at rationalizing our actions and blaming others that we often do not realize we are doing it. Society has trained us well in doing this. Clear messages are given: look out for yourself, put yourself first, indulge, don't feel guilty, and so on. We convince ourselves that we do no wrong; it is always the other person's fault. There is always a "because clause" or a "but factor." Someone else is always to blame and in this blame, we find anger, resentment, frustration, and sometimes violence.

However, the Lord's Prayer gives us another message: "Forgive us...as we forgive." Notice the two parts: (1) we sin and (2) we must forgive others. These words completely contradict society's messages of self-indulgence and self-preservation. This prayer is very challenging. It is not easy to forgive those who have hurt us. Sometimes it is even harder to admit that we have done wrong.

For this challenge, Lewis relied on prayer that helped him to "forgive for the moment." When he found himself having "to go on forgiving, to forgive the same offence again every time it recurs to the memory," he would run into a bit of a "tussle." As you may recall, for this challenge, he said that he would call to mind an offence of his own that was similar to an offence committed against him that he needed to forgive. For example, in praying for and trying to forgive those who bullied him at school, he would call to mind those whom he had bullied and hurt.[22]

Here, Lewis shows us how we can push beyond the negative feelings of anger, frustration, and hurt. In prayer and forgiveness, we find healing actions that will lead us to peace. He further demonstrates this with Doctor Cornelius and Caspian.

On top of the tower, Doctor Cornelius tells Caspian, "It is you Telmarines who silenced the beasts and the trees and the fountains, and who killed and drove away the Dwarfs and Fauns, and are now trying to cover up even the memory of them."[23] Clearly, Doctor Cornelius was hurt and affected by the Telmarines' actions. He could very well lash out at Caspian, a Telmarine, in revenge and anger. However, he does not and instead educates Caspian and asks for his help.

Caspian, feeling a tremendous amount of guilt, first responds, "I'm—I'm sorry, Doctor." Then, like us, he begins to squirm with, "It wasn't my fault, you know."[24] Wisely, Doctor Cornelius realizes that in his feelings of sorrow and guilt, Caspian is attempting to shift blame. He also knows that nothing productive will come from trying to allocate blame, only anger and hate.

Changes need to happen and pointing fingers will not help. That was not why Doctor Cornelius shared the stories with Caspian. He needed someone with whom to share his stories and he knew that Caspian also loved "the Old Things."[25] He did not intend to stir guilty feelings; he wanted Caspian's help and it worked. Caspian eventually responded, "How can I help?"[26]

Personal Ponderings

The story of how a young woman was murdered in a small midwestern town displays the community battlefield of love and hate. In an online forum of the newspaper reporting this story, someone displayed a picture of a lynched person in an attempt to link the murder with race. The newspaper found the picture within a matter of minutes and deleted it, but the damage had already been done. The murder has now been turned into a racial issue as the person who posted it had intended. While the crime had nothing to do with race, the community member placed blame on the murderer's race and stirred further feelings of anger and hate.

In an effort to diffuse the situation and find healing, the family of the victim has come forward to testify that the crime was not a racial crime. They do not want the incident to perpetuate any more pain and hate than already has come forth. In love, they have publicly forgiven the murderer. They demonstrate what Jesus has called us to do: to love our enemies. Their actions give us a much better image and hopefully will replace the image and message of the posted picture.

Unfortunately, this type of situation occurs much too often. People love to spread hostility and discord. For some reason it is more fun to talk about the bad and the ugly, than it is to talk about the good. The media capitalizes on this fact. More newspapers are sold when juicy gossip is reported because that type of news attracts interest and readers. It often becomes the topic of conversation. Focusing on the mistakes of others diverts the attention from ourselves. It gives a false sense of security. They must be worse than us. However, what we fail to see is that it creates a chain reaction. The more discord we spread, the more likely we will also be the victim of anger, hatred, and hostility.

How often did you solve your problem by yelling at someone? When did physical violence toward someone ever solve a problem? Honestly, have you ever felt better after gossiping about someone? Haven't all of these attempted solutions only perpetuated more hate, anger, and suffering?

Finding Purpose

When have you pointed the finger at someone else when you were guilty?

Why?

When have you retaliated in anger and hurt?

What was the result?

When have you responded in love and forgiveness?

What was the result?

What is hardest for you to forgive?

Why?

How might it help if you took Lewis's advice and thought of a time when you were guilty of a similar offense?

Finding Scripture

When we read Luke 6 and Matthew 5, a sense of culture shock may emerge by the message the scriptures tell us. We are very much a self-centered culture; we often think in terms of what we are entitled to and become irritated with those who get in the way of what we feel we deserve. However, in Luke 6:27–36 and Matthew 5:38–48, Jesus tells us to love those who hurt us. We are to give more to those who want to take from us. When someone strikes us, we are not told to defend ourselves. We are told to offer them the other cheek to strike. When we read these verses, we begin to feel the challenge that often put Lewis into a tussle. It is not easy, and we will not find support for this teaching in our secular culture.

> ## Suggested Scripture Reading and Reflections
>
> Read Luke 6:27–36 and Matthew 5:38–48 and take note of how Jesus's teachings still go against the grain of popular culture. Also, note the similarities and differences of the two passages.
>
> Why do you think that popular culture still has not embraced Jesus's teachings on love?
>
> What message does popular culture give us about love?
>
> Why do you think Jesus calls us to love our enemies?
>
> Why does forgiveness have to be discussed with love?
>
> Why does reading the two passages together give you a more complete understanding of what Jesus is calling us to do?

Holy Giftedness

Reflections on Lewis with Caspian

*W*hile we know Lewis as a talented and gifted writer, many have come to admire him even more for his other gifts. In reading the enormous volumes of letters he wrote through the course of his life, we see the many people he put before himself. While studying and preparing for exams, he never failed to write at least one letter a week to his friend Arthur Greeves. In those long letters, he encourages him with his readings, writings, and daily struggles.

In addition, in the letters and the introductions of the books of letters, we learn that when his wartime friend, Paddy Moore, perished in battle, he took on the responsibility of caring for Paddy's mother and sister. As shown in the letters, this was not an easy feat because of Mrs. Moore's demanding nature and need for constant attention. In fact, in many instances, Lewis performed duties of a house servant. His brother Warren describes her as "notably domineering and possessive by temperament" and goes on to say his brother's life with Mrs. Moore:

> cut down to a minimum his visits to his father, inter-fered constantly with his work, and imposed upon him a heavy burden of minor domestic tasks.... Nevertheless he continued in this restrictive and distracting servitude for many of his most fruitful years, suffering the worries of expense of repeated moves....[27]

Taking care of such a woman, when we know that Lewis did not like to be "interfered with,"[28] shows the gift of spiritual greatness.

Lewis also displayed the ability to put others before himself in his devoted responses to his fans. In *Letters to Children,* we get a sense of his ardent and fervent responses. They were not the scripted and generic letters that fans might receive today. They were handwritten, heartfelt, and reflective. He devoted large portions of every day to responding to the hundreds of letters he received—to his dying day. His brother Warren and friend Walter Hooper both attest to this devotion, as each of them helped him with this task in his later years of poor health.

We also see unselfish love when Lewis, late in life (1957), marries a woman suffering from cancer at her hospital bedside, knowing that she would need constant care and would soon die. For three years, Lewis had wedded bliss despite the illness.[29] Somewhat ironically, her name was Joy. (*Surprised by Joy* was published in 1955.) He tells us he found great happiness, and thus we see his marriage as a gift that requires a bravery of heart for he embraces a happiness that he knows he will soon grieve.

How does he do all of this? Only through the grace of God. While his conversion also came later in life (1931), God was beside him in all of these experiences, guiding him and leading him home, knowing that all of Lewis's experiences would one day be redirected and used for good. Hooper attests to this in *They Stand Together.* In reflecting on the years prior to Lewis's conversion, he says: "The hard knocks he had given and received as an atheist were later to serve as some of the finest weaponry he was to use in his long and spectacular career as a Christian apologist."[30]

Personal Ponderings

Lewis embeds this notion of gifts in *The Lion, the Witch and the Wardrobe*, and then brings it back again in *Prince Caspian*. In doing this, Lewis brings us to reflect on our own spiritual gifts—those obvious, not so obvious, and those forgotten.

When Peter, Susan, and Lucy dust off their forgotten gifts at the end of chapter 2, we gaze over at Edmund. Surely he must feel left out that he did not have a gift from Aslan. Nothing is said to remind us that Edmund was with the White Witch when the gifts were given. True to their word, Edmund's siblings left Edmund's betrayal in the past behind them.

As we continue to read further on, we may think about how quick we are to judge others and expect the worst. Poor Edmund, we are so hard on him for siding with the White Witch. Perhaps that is why Lewis redeems Edmund in *Prince Caspian* and has Aslan give Edmund the gift of "greatness."

The Gift of Greatness

We see Edmund through new eyes as he approaches the army of Miraz in chapter 13. We are told that "the other boys at Edmund's school" would not have "recognized him" either "if they had seen him at that moment. For Aslan had breathed on him at their meeting and a kind of greatness hung about him."[31] In this book, Edmund receives another gift. He does not betray his siblings. In fact, he gets beyond his own weaknesses and becomes great.

Lewis's Christian parallels are particularly striking. Aslan's breathing "greatness" on Edmund seems reminiscent of what is celebrated during the sacrament of confirmation. The one who is confirmed receives the gifts of the Holy Spirit. That person is called to be a witness to the faith just as Jesus breathed on his disciples after the resurrection with the words: "Receive the Holy Spirit" (John 20:22). The Holy Spirit breathes a whole new life into us at confirmation, transforms us, and gives us a kind of greatness.

Tired and Weak

Have you ever experienced one of those moments when you are exhausted? Not just tired but also exhausted and then, just as you feel you are about to collapse, you find yourself called on to perform yet one more task? You think to yourself, "I just can't, not today."

You have no idea how you are going to do it, but you do. Not only did you accomplish it, but also you did it so well that you actually amazed yourself. When you look back at this experience, there is only one explanation. You did it through the grace of God and with the help of the Holy Spirit.

Simple Tasks—Great Results

Sometimes when a family member suffers a serious health crisis, the rest of the family is challenged to do simple, small, and menial tasks as ways to meet the pressing needs of the situation. In addition to our ordinary work and family responsibilities, this may mean finding the strength to be flexible with adjusting personal schedules, taking on additional work such as feeding a sick relative at the hospital, compassionately listening to another in their time of illness, or accompanying an individual during therapy while that person is on the road to recovery. It means being there for another, which can be a very draining experience, both physically and emotionally.

The familiar words "with the grace of God and the help of the Holy Spirit" remind us that we are able to act and think beyond ourselves. Like Edmund, we have been breathed with a kind of greatness that allows us to go beyond ourselves especially when we may feel a sense of fatigue and weakness.

The Holy Spirit works in this way, burning inside us and traveling through each of us to accomplish great tasks with limited resources. We just need to be willing to let the Holy Spirit do its work. Although we may be tired, and the task may seem small, tedious, and insignificant, the Holy Spirit accomplishes greatness. The Holy Spirit works and ministers through us. Although we may be weak, tired, and unprepared, the Holy Spirit does great things.

Finding Purpose

How did your confirmation transform you?

When have you seen a kind of greatness working in someone?

When has the Holy Spirit worked through your tired and weakened body?

How can you be more aware of the Holy Spirit working in you and around you?

Finding Scripture

When we doubt our abilities to perform the tasks God places before us, we can also find encouragement in the story of Moses. When God appeared to him in a burning bush and asked Moses to deliver God's people out of Egypt, Moses did not exactly jump at the opportunity. Feeling rather inadequate in his abilities, Moses shrank from God's request. He presented several excuses as to why he would not be successful especially since he was a fugitive from Pharaoh. Why would they listen to me? Why would they believe you sent me? How will they understand me? "I am slow of speech and tongue."

Can you hear yourself here? Are you making excuses about why you cannot do what God asks?

God does not accept Moses's excuses, nor does he accept ours. He patiently questions Moses in return: "Who gives speech to mortals? Who makes them mute or deaf, seeing or blind? Is it not I, the Lord? Now go, and I will be with your mouth and teach you what you are to speak" (Exod 4:11–13). In this passage, God addresses not only Moses but also us. We need not fear about completing the tasks placed before us or question why they are given to us. God has his reasons and gives us what we need to do what he asks of us.

Lewis, who also tried to avoid God through much of his life with questions and excuses, found that putting off God was useless. Like Moses, Lewis found that God would not argue. "He only said, 'I am the Lord'; 'I am that I am'; 'I am'"[32] (Exod 3:14). While Moses and Lewis came to accept this, they found it to be a long and hard struggle with themselves. Lewis describes his surrender as "a prodigal who is brought in kicking, struggling, resentful, and darting his eyes in every direction for a chance of escape."[33] Moses is also presented similarly. After acknowledging that he is indeed talking to God, he uses every excuse he can think of to escape God's call for him—even after seeing his staff turn into a snake and back to a staff again and his hand becoming leprous and then healing. However, are we not the same?

God performs miracle after miracle for us including the ultimate death and resurrection of his Son. We still try to hide from God and find reasons why we should not do what he asks of us. Instead of rejoicing in the gifts that he gives to us, we hide in our perceived failures and inadequacies.

> ### Suggested Scripture Reading and Reflections
>
> Read Exodus 3:4—4:17 and consider the gifts God has given you and what he is calling you to do.
>
> When have you come face to face with God?
> What was your reaction?
> When have you made excuses to God and focused on what you thought were inadequacies?
> What gifts have you hidden or forgotten?
> What gifts might God be calling you to use now?
> What excuses are you making?
> Why?

Gifted Gender

Reflections of Lewis with Caspian

*I*t was not until late in life that Lewis found the woman that he would marry. She brought him great joy, which ironically was her name. One has to wonder, if that is not why he titled his autobiography *Surprised by Joy.* In commenting on his relationship with Joy to a friend, he said, "I never expected to have, in my sixties, the happiness that passed me by in my twenties." Regarding their relationship, Warren remarks that "to his friends who saw them together it was clear that they not only loved but were in love with each other."[34]

In describing his brother's wife, Warren says that she was "witty, intellectually stimulating, fun, an excellent conversationalist, well-read, Christian, and in emanating all of these qualities she was intensely feminine." Additionally, he remarks that in Joy his brother finally found "the only woman whom he had met (although his letters show, he had known with great affection many able women) who had a brain which matched his own suppleness, in width of interest, in analytical grasp, and above all in humour and sense of fun."[35]

In Lewis's relationship, we see how God intended male and female to complement each other. They brought each other great joy and comfort. Even more remarkably, they found this in the midst of great illness for Joy was dying of cancer when they married "not in church but at the bride's bedside in the Wingfield Hospital."[36] Despite the cancer they did enjoy three happy years together in which Joy became even well enough to travel to Ireland and Greece for what Lewis described to Greeves as "a belated honeymoon."[37] Warren labels that period of his brother's life as "a short episode, of glory and tragedy: for Jack, the total (though heartbreaking) fulfillment of a whole dimension to his nature that had previously been starved and thwarted."[38] Truly, Lewis had been surprised by Joy!

However, while the union of Joy and Lewis shows how complimentary the union of male and female can be and how God intended them to be, society also has shown many instances where male and female are at odds. At times, this conflict and fighting over gender roles, causes great discord and disharmony.

In *The Four Loves*, Lewis deals with this issue in his chapter on friendship. There he explains that when a male and a female enter into a relationship on different levels, they simply cannot work compatibly with one another. One spends much time trying to bring the other one up to their level while the other resents trying to be made into what he or she cannot and does not want to be.

He also has found it essential for the sexes to spend time together in friendship. Males need to spend time with other males and females need to spend time with other females. When one tries to invade the other's circle and control it, misery follows. He finds it natural and necessary to laugh and not understand the need for the opposite sex to get together and act silly. For example, it is acceptable for women to want to shop and for men to want to watch football. We do not need to understand it. Lewis finds this type of behavior necessary and "healthy that each should have a lively sense of the other's absurdity" for "humanity is tragic-comical; but the division of the sexes enables each to see in the other the joke that often escapes it in itself—and the pathos too."[39]

In *Prince Caspian,* we get a comical look at how our gender battles play out even in children. When the children are looking for Aslan's How and not finding it, Edmund and Lucy begin to snip at each other. Of course, like us, this snipping turns into a verbal battle about gender when Susan remarks, "I can't remember all that at all," and Edmund tells Peter and the Dwarf, "That's the worst of girls. They never carry a map in their heads." Lucy, rightfully angered by Edmund's gloating and stereotypical remark, banters back, "That's because our heads have something inside them."[40]

Both Lucy and Edmund lash out at each other here because they are frustrated. Unfortunately, they expose their hidden hostilities about gender conflicts. Lewis allows us to look at ourselves here. Do we not also toss out these types of remarks to the opposite sex? While somewhat comical, they also can be hurtful and perpetuate a vicious cycle of division between male and female.

Stealing My Talents

As a parent, I am constantly in the midst of the type of verbal bantering portrayed by Edmund and Lucy. My son and daughters still have not realized how to come together in harmony. Instead, they feel threatened by each other's differences in gender. The constant argument is over who is better at sports. At the young age of three, I began hearing them shout at each other, "You are trying to steal my talents."

The battle still wages. My daughter is frustrated that she cannot play baseball, and my son worries that she will one day invade his territory. Wanting to prove her abilities, she has excelled in every sport she has played. Comically, my son has gravitated to the only area she cannot enter.

This frustrates me on a daily basis after doing everything in my power to dispel gender stereotypes in my children. It is very challenging. Society constantly depicts and bombards images of what male and female should be and how we should act toward one another. Unfortunately, the image is usually the same. The female must be valued for her appearance and lure whereas the male must be the stronger, smarter, and more powerful. Victoria's Secret is perhaps one of the worst advertisers of this point, and this type of stereotypical message is often found in many other commercials and advertisements. These messages are out to create and perpetuate the dominance of one sex over the other. If we are ever to find peace and harmony, we must learn to love and respect each other as we were intended. Lewis and Joy found a completeness in each other. Is this not what God intended?

Ironically, the children only get further away from Aslan's How as they banter with one another both physically and symbolically. Aslan chooses the youngest, a girl, to lead the children to him. Prejudiced and reflecting only on her age and gender, they choose to ignore her pleas for them to follow her. They simply do not believe her. As a result, they remain lost much longer than necessary.

Isn't Lewis making a valid point here? Do we not also miss finding him when we are blinded by our own gender prejudices and stereotypes? Was there a reason that Lewis did not find bliss and happiness in a companion until late in life, not long after he also had found his spiritual joy? What joy are we also missing in continuing to perpetuate and focus on division between the sexes?

Finding Purpose

When have you found the type of happiness in the opposite sex that Lewis found with Joy?

What made you so compatible?

How did you avoid gender conflicts?

What causes gender conflicts in your life?

How can you avoid them?

How does the media and advertising benefit from perpetuating gender conflict?

What can we do to build a healthy rapport of love and respect between the sexes?

Do you agree with what Lewis said about males and females in *The Four Loves?*

Why or why not?

Finding Scripture

Chapters 1—11 from the book of Genesis are often referred to as mythical in the sense that their purpose seems to be to help us understand good and bad and our relationship with God. In Genesis 1 and 2, we see that God created male and female in one flesh to complement one another. He looked at his creation as very good. It was not until they ate from the tree of knowledge of good and evil that division occurred. Today, we also create division with knowledge, as we seek to grow in knowledge so that we can be smarter, stronger, and more powerful than one another.

Suggested Scripture Reading and Reflections

Read Genesis 1:24–31 and Genesis 2:20–25 and reflect on how male and female complement one another.

Why were male and female created?

What does it mean to be created of one flesh?

Genesis 2:20–25 is one of the most common readings at weddings. Why?

How does knowledge continue to divide us?

How can we work to live with each other as were intended?

What role does love play in this?

NOTES

Section One

1. C. S. Lewis, *Surprised by Joy: The Shape of My Early Life* (New York: A Harvest Book, Harcourt Inc., 1955), 7.

2. Ibid., 16.

3. Ibid.

4. Ibid.

5. Ibid., 10.

6. C. S. Lewis, *The Chronicles of Narnia* (New York: HarperCollins Publishers, 2001), 337.

7. Ibid.

8. Ibid., 338.

9. Ibid.

10. Ibid.

11. Ibid.

12. Ibid., 339.

13. C. S. Lewis, *Surprised by Joy,* 216.

14. Ibid., 221.

15. Ibid., 220.

16. Ibid., 221.

17. C. S. Lewis, *The Chronicles of Narnia,* 373.

18. C. S. Lewis, *Surprised by Joy,* 223.

19. Ibid., 225.

20. Ibid.

21. Ibid., 226.

22. Ibid., 227.

23. Ibid., 184.

24. Ibid.

25. C. S. Lewis, *The Chronicles of Narnia*, 373.

26. Lyle W. Dorsett and Marjorie Lamp Mead, eds., *C. S. Lewis: Letters to Children* (New York: Macmillan Publishing Company, 1985), 26.

27. C. S. Lewis, *Surprised by Joy*, 191.

28. Ibid., 178.

29. Ibid., 179.

30. Ibid.

31. Ibid., 179–80.

32. Ibid., 179–81.

33. Ibid., 15.

34. Ibid.

35. Ibid., 16.

36. Ibid., 17.

37. Ibid., 18–19.

38. Dorsett and Mead, *C. S. Lewis: Letters to Children*, 29.

39. Ibid., 52.

40. Ibid., 5.

41. Ibid., 31.

42. C. S. Lewis, *The Chronicles of Narnia*, 418.

43. Dorsett and Mead, *C. S. Lewis: Letters to Children*, 31.

44. C. S. Lewis, *Surprised by Joy*, 223.

45. Ibid., 172.

46. Ibid., 223.

47. Ibid., 224.

48. Ibid., 225.

49. Ibid., 224.

50. Ibid., 225.

51. Walter Hooper, ed., *They Stand Together: The Letters of C. S. Lewis to Arthur Greeves (1914–1963)* (New York: Macmillan Publishing Company, 1979), 64.

52. Ibid., 134–35.

53. Ibid., 135.

54. Ibid.

55. Ibid.

56. Ibid., 136.

57. Ibid., 138.

58. C. S. Lewis, *Surprised by Joy*, 116.

59. Ibid.

60. C. S. Lewis, *The Chronicles of Narnia*, 393.

61. "Amish Forgive, Pray and Mourn," *CBS News*, October 4, 2006, www.cbsnews.com/stories/2006/10/04/national/main 2059816.shtml.

62. C. S. Lewis, *The Chronicles of Narnia*, 393.

63. Luke Timothy Johnson, "The General Letters and Revelation," in *The Catholic Study Bible*, gen. ed. Donald Senior (New York: Oxford University Press, 1990), 572.

64. C. S. Lewis, *Surprised by Joy*, 227.

65. Ibid., 225–29.

66. W. H. Lewis, *Letters of C. S. Lewis* (London: The Chaucer Press, 1966), 32.

67. C. S. Lewis, *The Chronicles of Narnia*, 372.

68. W. H. Lewis, *Letters of C. S. Lewis*, 32.

69. C. S. Lewis, *Surprised by Joy*, 238.

70. C. S. Lewis, *The Chronicles of Narnia*, 411.

71. Ibid., 417.

72. W. H. Lewis, *Letters of C. S. Lewis*, 82–87.

73. Ibid., 101.

74. C. S. Lewis, *The Chronicles of Narnia*, 417.

Section Two

1. Hooper, *They Stand Together,* 200.

2. W.H. Lewis, *Letters of C. S. Lewis,* 38–40.

3. Ibid., 202.

4. Dorsett and Mead, *C. S. Lewis Letters to Children,* 111.

5. C. S. Lewis, *The Chronicles of Narnia,* 347.

6. C. S. Lewis, *Surprised by Joy,* 100.

7. Ibid., 106.

8. Ibid., 100.

9. Ibid., 96.

10. Ibid., 108.

11. Ibid., 107.

12. Ibid., 115.

13. Ibid.

14. Ibid., 119.

15. C. S. Lewis, *The Chronicles of Narnia,* 396.

16. "Virginia Tech Shooter Cho Seung-Hui Mails Manifesto to NBC News," *Post Chronicle,* April 18, 2007, http://www.postchronicle.com/cgi-bin/artman/exec/view.cgi?archive=14&num=75707.

17. N. R. Kleinfield, "Before Deadly Rage, a Life Consumed by Troubling Silence," *New York Times,* April 22, 2007, http://www.nytimes.com.

18. C. S. Lewis, *Letters to Malcolm: Chiefly on Prayer* (New York: Harcourt, Brace & World, 1963), 28.

19. C. S. Lewis, *The Chronicles of Narnia,* 380; emphasis added.

20. Ibid.

21. Ibid.

22. Ibid.

23. Ibid., 380–81.

24. Ibid., 381.

25. C. S. Lewis, *Letters to Malcolm,* 26.

26. Ibid., 27.

27. C. S. Lewis, *The Chronicles of Narnia,* 381.

28. Ibid.

29. Donald Senior, "The Gospel Accordiing to Matthew," in *The Catholic Study Bible,* gen. ed. Donald Senior (New York: Oxford Press, 1990), 3.

30. C. S. Lewis, *The Chronicles of Narnia,* 387.

31. C. S. Lewis, *Mere Christianity* (New York: The MacMillan Company, 1955), 104–6.

32. Ibid., 110–15.

33. C. S. Lewis, *The Chronicles of Narnia,* 356–57.

34. C. S. Lewis, *Mere Christianity,* 113.

35. Ibid., 58; emphasis added.

36. Ibid., 62–64.

37. Ibid., 64.

38. C. S. Lewis, *The Chronicles of Narnia,* 340.

39. Ibid., 343–44.

40. Ibid., 383.

41. Ibid., 384.

42. Ibid., 386.

43. Ibid., 340.

44. Ibid., 406.

45. Ibid., 407.

46. Ibid., 408.

47. Ibid.

48. Ibid., 409.

49. Ibid., 405.

50. Ibid., 405–6.

Section Three

1. C. S. Lewis, *Mere Christianity,* 23.

2. Ibid.

3. Ibid.

4. C. S. Lewis, *The Chronicles of Narnia,* 378.

5. Ibid., 385–86.

6. Ibid., 386.

7. C. S. Lewis, *Surprised by Joy,* 68.

8. C. S. Lewis, *The Chronicles of Narnia,* 412.

9. C. S. Lewis, *Mere Christianity,* 100–101.

10. C. S. Lewis, *Surprised by Joy,* 7.

11. C. S. Lewis, *The Four Loves* (New York: Harcourt, Inc., 1988), 20–21.

12. C. S. Lewis, *The Chronicles of Narnia,* 378–79.

13. C. S. Lewis, *Surprised by Joy,* 20–21.

14. Hooper, *They Stand Together,* 565.

15. C. S. Lewis, *The Chronicles of Narnia,* 410.

16. Hooper, *They Stand Together,* 566.

17. Ibid.

18. W. H. Lewis, *Letters of C. S. Lewis,* 24.

19. Hooper, *They Stand Together,* 31.

20. C. S. Lewis, *The Chronicles of Narnia,* 401–2.

21. C. S. Lewis, *Letters to Malcolm,* 34.

22. Ibid., 27–28.

23. C. S. Lewis, *The Chronicles of Narnia,* 338.

24. Ibid., 339.

25. Ibid.

26. Ibid.

27. W. H. Lewis, *Letters of C. S. Lewis,* 12.

28. C. S. Lewis, *Surprised by Joy,* 228.

29. W. H. Lewis, *Letters of C. S. Lewis,* 23.

30. Hooper, *They Stand Together,* 26.

31. C. S. Lewis, *The Chronicles of Narnia,* 399.

32. C. S. Lewis, *Surprised by Joy,* 227.

33. Ibid., 228.

34. W. H. Lewis, *Letters of C. S. Lewis,* 23.

35. Ibid.

36. Ibid.

37. Hooper, *They Stand Together,* 546.

38. W. H. Lewis, *Letters of C. S. Lewis,* 23.

39. C. S. Lewis. *The Four Loves,* 77.

40. C. S. Lewis, *The Chronicles of Narnia,* 370.

BIBLIOGRAPHY

Dorsett, Lyle W., and Marjorie Lamp Mead, eds. *C. S. Lewis: Letters to Children*. New York: Macmillan Publishing Company, 1985.

Hooper, Walter, ed. *They Stand Together: The Letters of C. S. Lewis to Arthur Greeves (1914–1963)*. New York: Macmillan Publishing Company, 1979.

Johnson, Luke Timothy. "The General Letters and Revelation." In *The Catholic Study Bible,* edited by Donald Senior, 572. New York: Oxford University Press, 1990.

Lewis, C. S. *The Chronicles of Narnia*. New York: HarperCollins Publishers, 2001.

————. *The Four Loves*. New York: Harcourt, Inc., 1988.

————. *Letters to Malcolm: Chiefly on Prayer.* New York: Harcourt Brace & World, 1963.

————. *Mere Christianity.* New York: The MacMillan Company, 1955.

————. *Surprised by Joy: The Shape of My Early Life*. New York: A Harvest Book, Harcourt Inc., 1955.

Lewis, W. H., ed. *Letters of C. S. Lewis*. London: The Chaucer Press, 1966.

Senior, Donald. "The Gospel According to Matthew." In *The Catholic Study Bible*, ed. Donald Senior, 3. New York: Oxford University Press, 1990.